THE
SURPRISING
POWER
OF NOT
KNOWING
WHAT TO DO

Discovering Creativity

and Compassion

in a Time of Chaos

Jay Gordon Cone, PhD

THE
SURPRISING
POWER
OF NOT
KNOWING
WHAT TO DO

UNSTUCK
MINDS
MEDIA™

Unstuck Minds Media is an imprint of Unstuck Minds, LLC. For more information: jay@unstuckminds.com and www.unstuckminds.com.

Library of Congress Control Number: 2020922947

First Paperback Edition January 2021

Consulting editor: Alan Rinzler
Copyeditor: Leslie Tilley
Cover design: Laura Duffy Design
Book design: Elina Cohen

ISBN 978-1-7359274-0-4 (paperback)
ISBN 978-1-7359274-1-1 (ebook)

For Katherine, Abigail, Hannah, and Rebekah

CONTENTS

PART THREE: FOUR DISCIPLINES FOR NAVIGATING CHAOS

PREFACE

This is not the book I intended to write. I can't tell you how many versions of this preface have come and gone. A preface should help the reader understand the author's relationship to the subject of the book and how the book came to be, so this piece has evolved in parallel with the book. This book started out as a set of ideas for helping organizational leaders navigate complex and uncertain conditions. It has been recast as an antidote to thinking that isolates, divides, limits, and misdirects.

I completed the manuscript during the summer of 2020—a year that reset the bar for what constitutes complex and uncertain conditions. My editor pointed out that what I had written for organizational leaders could not be a timelier message for anyone feeling overwhelmed and disoriented by the interlocking calamities of racial inequality, political turmoil, a pandemic, historic unemployment, and a climate crisis.

I'm good at thinking my way out of challenging situations. I can remove myself from confusion and anxiety while offering ideas for how to process the various aspects of a problem. It's a skill that makes me a successful facilitator, coach, and consultant. It's also a coping mechanism that protects me from getting emotionally embroiled in the situations my clients want help with. But when I can't come up with a way to think about something, I not only feel helpless, I start to feel inadequate.

As I contemplated an expanded mission for the book, my desire to make a difference started bumping up against my psychology. My editor was coaxing me onto a larger stage. Suddenly I felt overwhelmed and disoriented. I had just written a book about the upsides of not knowing what to do. Would I be able to take a dose of my own medicine?

ON MAY 25, 2020, a 46-year-old Black man named George Floyd, was murdered by white Minneapolis police officer Derek Chauvin. Lying in the street for 9 minutes and 30 seconds,[1] handcuffed, with his neck pinned under Chauvin's knee, Floyd begged for air and eventually suffocated to death. Chauvin crushed the life out of George Floyd with callous indifference. The video of George Floyd's murder shocked and enraged the world. Still, we wonder if the recent outcry for racial equity will reach a tipping point that leads to meaningful progress.

As I write in the closing months of 2020, surging numbers of people infected with Covid-19 may soon overwhelm our health care system. Meanwhile, the sitting president of the United States obsesses over his election loss, plots against the incoming administration, and undermines a smooth and peaceful transfer of power. Trust in democratic institutions is on the decline; conspiracy theories are on the rise.

We've lost the ability to think together because we can't agree on what constitutes factual information. We look at the same situation and draw opposing conclusions. Depending on the sources of information you trust, a person wearing a face covering might represent a responsible citizen or a brain-washed conformist. We have problems to solve, yet working together feels risky.

I'm in the business of helping people get unstuck. I've been hiding in organizations, busying myself with teaching leaders to notice and avoid thinking traps. It's work that helps me feel useful. Meanwhile, though, the world has been coming apart at the seams. Dare I turn my attention to more significant problems?

It's as if the universe has thrown down a gauntlet: You want to help people get unstuck? Let's see how you do with threats of a lethal pandemic, a climate crisis, deeply entrenched social injustice, and massive unemployment.

To be clear, I don't know what to do about the crises that have started to define the coming decade. I've spent my adult life ducking experiences that leave me vulnerable to feelings of helplessness and incompetence. I've focused on challenges inside organizations because it's an environment I understand well enough to be of use. I needed someone else, a wise and insistent editor, to point out the obvious. I had written that in chaotic times, one should be skeptical of expertise rooted in the past. I claimed that not knowing what to do could be liberating rather than paralyzing. Yet I felt stymied by an invitation to help people trying to make progress on our most consequential problems because I lacked expertise and didn't know how to help.

Even if I wanted to ignore the world's problems and remain focused on organizations, the twin viruses of racism and Covid-19 do not respect arbitrary distinctions between personal life and work life. Boomers and Gen-Xers were raised to believe that bringing our full, unfiltered selves to the workplace was inappropriate and counterproductive. Don't discuss religion or politics at work was the unwritten law. But over the last few years, the workplace has been undergoing a transformation. A socially engaged and interconnected generation of workers have refused to sublimate their values and ideals to corporate goals.

Since the beginning of the 21st century, terrorism, wars, mass shootings, natural disasters, cyberattacks, and other horrors have darkened our mood and tested our idealism. Until recently, I've managed to separate my exasperation about the state of the world from my responsibilities to my clients. Now, external world issues have become internal organizational priorities. During the 2016 presidential campaign Hillary Clinton introduced the term *implicit bias* to the general public. Two years later, two Black men in a Philadelphia Starbucks were inappropriately handcuffed and arrested for trespassing. In response to the outcry that followed, Starbucks shut down thousands of stores and put all their employees through racial bias training. Hillary Clinton's raising concerns about implicit bias may not have roused my clients, but Starbucks closing its

4

stores got corporate America's attention. Walling ourselves off
from our shameful history could no longer keep uncomfortable truths and disturbing events on the periphery. The dam
was set to burst when Derek Chauvin brazenly crushed the life
out of George Floyd.

Not surprisingly, at Unstuck Minds my business partner,
Lisa Weaver, and I have been getting requests to help organizations and their leaders learn how to acknowledge and respond to unconscious bias and racism in our society. I've read
the books, listened to the podcasts, and watched the videos. As
a white male I have not, however, lived the oppression. I don't
experience the unrelenting dissonance between the promise
of liberty and justice for all and the reality of being devalued because of my race. When clients ask for help combating
racism and other adverse effects of implicit bias, I am neither
neutral nor an expert.

It's not just issues of race exposing my vulnerabilities these
days. In the midst of the Covid-19 pandemic, our firm has
been getting requests to help leaders learn how to manage distributed workers who may never again return to daily office
jobs. When it comes to a world where convening is dangerous,
no one is unaffected. And when it comes to reinventing work
for that world, no one has expertise.

I remember feeling similarly incapacitated as I watched the
election returns of 2016. At first, I wasn't focused on what
a Donald Trump presidency would usher in. I was too busy
struggling to understand how I could have been so out of
touch with American voters. I consider myself well-informed
and broad-minded. It made me wonder what other erroneous

assumptions I've been harboring. I can recover from the sting of being wrong if I get to learn something from it, but the 2016 presidential election pulled the rug out from under me. I wasn't just mistaken; my thinking was flawed. I've heard all the theories and still can't make them add up.

I am not by nature a pessimist. In fact, I've gotten pretty good at spinning our global dilemmas as necessary corrections that will eventually lead to an era of collaborative and humanistic social structures. I am not writing this book to explain what's going on, nor am I offering solutions. My purpose is to suggest practices that help us adapt to chaos and instability and allow us to meet the uncertainty of the moment with compassion and creativity.

When I was challenged to expand the scope of my work and the audience for this book, I first hesitated, and then rediscovered the surprising power of not knowing what to do. I'm now even more convinced that my reflex to turn away from a problem because I don't know what to do takes a toll on my creativity. And if I only work with people who think like I do, my compassion atrophies like an unused muscle.

Do you know how a vaccine works? A vaccine doesn't eliminate the disease or cure those who have been infected. A vaccine trains the immune system to make us less susceptible to a disease. Recent events have infected us with a malaise against which we need inoculation. It feels as though the foundations of civil society that anchor our identities and our aspirations have come unmoored. When our bedrock assumptions are threatened, we become susceptible to arrogant leaders, conspiracy theorists, and purveyors of snake oil. Adrift, we are grateful for any port in a storm. We look outside ourselves for answers—any answers—when what we need is a way to fortify our ability to access creativity and compassion amid the turbulence.

This book is not a prescription for what ails us but more like a fitness routine for thinking and feeling. You'll read about techniques that protect you and those you serve from becoming paralyzed by limited and misguided thinking.

Just because I decided to write a book about responding to political and social turmoil doesn't mean I'm sharing my reactions to current events. Whether you're put off or drawn in by partisan commentary, don't expect to read about my take on current events. Instead, many of the examples and stories in this book are drawn from decades of experience helping leaders and their organizations overcome challenges and pursue opportunities. But leaders aren't the only people who become stuck.

The book opens with insights into how and why we get stuck. Part Two makes the counterintuitive claim that in uncertain times, focusing on *what to do* limits creativity and compassion. Part Three describes four thinking disciplines that, when consistently practiced, help us form insights and discover options even in turbulent and chaotic times.

I wrote this book for people who are feeling disoriented and stuck. I invite you to embrace the surprising power of not knowing what to do—to become not *like* a beginner but to become a true beginner, one who can see abundant possibilities because you are no longer a captive of assumptions the world has left behind.

PART ONE

THE NATURE OF OUR INABILITY TO DEAL WITH CHAOS

A time of turbulence is a dangerous time, but its greatest danger is a temptation to deny reality.

—Peter Drucker, *Managing in Turbulent Times*

1 /

Redefining Problems

My wife Katherine and I have three daughters. When our daughters lived at home, they shared a bathroom situated between two bedrooms. Our oldest daughter, Abby, had her own bedroom on one side of the bathroom. Our middle daughter Hannah and her younger sister Bekah shared a bedroom on the other side of the bathroom. There are two doors leading into the bathroom, one from each of the bedrooms, and two sinks in the bathroom, one per bedroom.

In real estate jargon, this arrangement is referred to as a "Jack and Jill" bathroom, although in our case it was more of a "Jill and Jill (and Jill)" situation. As teenagers, two of our three daughters wore little to no makeup and did not spend much time caring for their nails. Hannah, on the other hand accumulated cosmetics, nail polishes, and other beautification equipment I'm too unfamiliar with to name. An image sums it up.

My daughters' bathroom counter.

Note that the basin is stained with mascara goo. A random roll of toilet paper is positioned near a dangerously hot electric hair device, which is not in use but plugged in. There's a water bottle near two tubes of toothpaste. Apparently, the exertion involved in using all this stuff requires periodic hydration.

You could say that Katherine and I felt stuck. We didn't like the condition of the bathroom, but complaining, cajoling, and demanding resulted only in small, temporary improvements, followed by a return to the condition in the photograph. (By the way, our daughters are grown and no longer living at home, so the situation I'm describing is now someone else's problem.)

I mention the situation with the messy bathroom because it illustrates an important point about problems. David Straus, the founder of Interaction Associates and the author of *How to Make Collaboration Work*, defines a problem as "a situation someone wants to change." [1] By this definition, when it comes to collaborating with my daughter on cleaning up the bathroom, only one of us has a problem. In other words, only one of us has a situation he wants to change.

Perhaps you're thinking that a more authoritarian approach to getting my daughter to clean her bathroom was called for. Let's say, for example, that I told Hannah she'd get her phone back when the bathroom was clean. I have then created a situation my daughter is motivated to change. Applying Straus's definition, *she* has a problem to solve. Notice, however, that Hannah would not be solving the problem I want solved. Instead, she'd be working on the problem of getting her phone back—whereas I'm more interested in her making progress on showing respect for other family members. Consequently, I shouldn't be surprised if Hannah succeeded in solving her problem but in the long run didn't really solve my problem.

For the purposes of this book, feeling stuck is being dissatisfied with your current situation and not knowing what to do about it. Of course, it's possible to be stuck and not realize it until you become aware of some preferable situation. Either way, the experience of being stuck starts with a tension or disequilibrium. When someone who feels stuck has an insight that leads to new options, the tension is resolved and that person becomes unstuck. The disciplines described in this book are ways to avoid getting stuck as well as ways to improve your situation when you feel stuck.

Here's how Katherine and I might have benefitted from this book when we felt stuck about how to encourage our daughter to keep her bathroom clean. One telltale sign that people are stuck is that they ask the wrong question about the situation they want to change. For example, asking ourselves how to get Hannah to keep her bathroom clean and organized turns out to be a question that just makes things worse. A better question is how do we reduce the amount of nagging at home. The question is better because it's derived from an insight about our situation that opens up options we didn't consider. One important goal of this book is to help people learn how to turn ordinary, unproductive questions into questions that invite new options.

BEFORE WE CAN learn how to avoid being paralyzed by chaos and uncertainty, we need a better understanding of how we become paralyzed in the first place. The first step is to make a distinction between *thinking traps,* or errors in the way we process information, and *feeling traps,* a counterproductive influence of emotions.

Thinking traps relate to the way our prefrontal cortex (specifically the dorsolateral prefrontal cortex)—the part of the brain that controls our working memory and selective attention—gets involved when we need to solve problems, make decisions, or regulate our behavior. Feeling traps show up when our limbic system steps in. The limbic system supports our emotional life, including our reactions to situations we perceive as threatening. When we miss information or misinterpret information, insights elude us. When our emotions protect us from the discomfort of change, new options feel more like hazards and less like solutions. Without insights and options, we stay stuck.

Thinking traps create blind spots. We have the physical experience of a blind spot when an object disappears from sight, like the car slightly behind you in the next lane that you can't see until you turn your head. Because we have blind spots, there could be something in our visual field that we don't notice. In the same way, cognitive blind spots cause us to miss data and information we need to make judgments and solve problems. Some cognitive blind spots, called *inattentional blindness,* cause us to miss things because once we aim our attention at one thing, other things seem to become invisible. If we didn't have inattentional blindness, magic would not be entertaining, and pickpockets would be less successful.

Other blind spots in our thinking relate to the way we process information; they are known as cognitive biases. The term *cognitive bias* and much of the original research on the subject got started in the 1970s with the work of two social scientists, Amos Tversky and Daniel Kahneman.[2] Researchers and practitioners have catalogued dozens of cognitive biases. You can find a list by visiting Wikipedia, but be forewarned, it's a little depressing to read through all the flaws in our ability to make sound judgments.

In the chapters that follow, we'll be learning about two blind spots that conspire to limit the information we process, which in turn explain a lot about what keeps us stuck. The first, *confirmation bias,* is perhaps the most well-known and per-nicious of our cognitive biases. The second, *need for closure*[3] is a less well-known feature of human cognition. It acts less like a blindness to information and more like a tendency to disregard additional information.

What I call feeling traps are related to, and sometimes the cause of, our thinking traps. Thinking traps refer to the flaws in the way we process information. Feeling traps show up when we unconsciously protect ourselves from experiencing negative emotions—emotions that we may need to process before we can get unstuck.

As with cognitive blind spots, we are not conscious of the influences of feeling traps. Some social psychologists use the term *implicit emotion regulation*[4] to refer to the unconscious processes that influence our emotional responses. To simplify things, I'll refer to feeling traps as threats. I'm using the term *threats* because the feeling traps that keep us stuck are responsible for mental processes that protect us from experiencing harm. In the chapters that follow, I will review research about how we deal with the threat of losing something and about our unconscious strategies to avoid situations that make us anxious. In other words, I hope to clarify why it feels safer to cling to the status quo than to reach for a breakthrough.

And why wouldn't we want the safety of the status quo? Haven't we had enough turbulence and uncertainty to satisfy even the most adventurous among us? I'm in the business of helping people reach for breakthroughs. Normally, I work with groups to ferret out their thinking and feeling traps. I then nudge them out of their comfort zones in search of novel options. This year I'm learning to tread lightly.

If forced to assert a political identity, I would describe myself as progressive. Progressives want change; that's literally what it means to be progressive. I have a suggestion for progressives who value self-improvement and feel desperate for a silver lining amid today's chaos: Take a moment to reflect on what it feels like to want some predictability and clarity back in your life. Hold onto that feeling and reconnect with it the next time you get impatient with someone who stubbornly clings to the status quo. As for me, the next time I push for a breakthrough, I will be in a much better position to empathize with what I'm asking of people. Standing still is not an option, but we shouldn't be shocked by people digging in their heels. Pushing people to endorse substantive change while remaining indifferent to their blind spots and threats is counterproductive.

Let's start with a story about how blind spots and threats collude to keep us stuck.

2 /

Are You Ever Surprised by How Often You're Right?

Eli Rittman manages sales reps in the Pacific Northwest for a global consumer packaged goods company headquartered in Portland, Oregon. Eli is stuck, but he doesn't realize it—not until he is confronted with the news that a member of his team named Jeff, whom he neither respects nor trusts, has just been promoted. What's worse, Jeff is now Eli's new boss.

An all-company email greeted employees reporting to work on Monday morning with news of the promotion: Jeff Schaefer, formerly the sales manager for the Midwest region, has been named executive vice president of sales for the Americas. Having picked up the email on his phone before he reached the elevator, Eli bypassed his own office and, without bothering to remove his coat, charged into the office of his trusted colleague Molly Lassiter. Closing the door, he stands across the desk from her, and before Molly can shift her attention from the computer screen, he asks with a mix of exasperation and disgust, "What the hell are they thinking?"

ELI REPRESENTS AN amalgam of leaders I've met in my work as a consultant. To understand why the news of Jeff's promotion frustrates and disorients Eli, we first need to understand the role confirmation bias plays in how all of us, including Eli, take in and process information. Confirmation bias is the tendency to interpret new information as evidence that our existing beliefs are true.

According to social psychologist Scott Plous, the term *confirmation bias* was coined by the English psychologist Peter Wason.[1] Wason conducted experiments in the 1960s to study how biases influence our ability to reason. About a decade later, and to help illustrate how thought processes become self-reinforcing, Chris Argyris, a Harvard professor and pioneer in the field of organizational development, created a model called the Ladder of Inference.[2]

Argyris used the image of a ladder to describe the architecture of abstraction, in which we move from specific data to generalized beliefs about the world. As we process information about something we experience, we metaphorically move up the ladder.

At the bottom of our ladders of inference is sensory data. As we move up the ladder, we select data to pay attention to, we add meaning to the data, we make assumptions and draw conclusions about the data, and with repeated experience we form beliefs about the situations we encounter as we compare new situations to prior experience. At the top of this ladder, we take action based on our beliefs. A key feature of the model is the relationship between the generalized beliefs we have formed and the data we select from any situation that gets our attention. The Ladder of Inference model represents confirmation bias as a loop from the generalized beliefs at the top of the ladder to the first rung of the ladder where we select data to focus on from what is available to us. Let's consider an example before we return to Eli and his reaction to the news that Jeff Schaefer is his new boss.

Suppose you believe that drivers in Boston are aggressive and eagerly honk their horns to give you feedback on your driving. One day you find yourself driving in Boston waiting at a red light. The light turns green and the driver behind you honks his horn.

Confirmation bias predicts that you will ascribe characteristics and motives to the driver that reinforce your belief about Boston drivers. Using the Ladder of Inference framework, we could say that you selected the data of the sound of the horn and then mentally processed your way up the ladder to reach a conclusion. You noticed the horn, but you missed the Kansas license plate clearly visible in your rearview mirror. The fact that the driver in this case is not from Boston doesn't matter. You're not inclined in that moment to give him the benefit of the doubt. You're also not motivated to seek out alternative explanations.

If the same thing happened in a different city, you might assume that the driver behind you is late for work or trying to get the attention of someone in the next lane—or visiting from Boston. Because we aren't always aware of our beliefs, we don't recognize how our beliefs might be influencing the information we pay attention to. Since our ability to pay attention to data has limitations, we favor the data our belief system prepares us to notice. The information we pick out from our daily interactions with the world often strengthens what we already believe is true.

Have you ever marveled at how often you seem to be right about things? When you compare the amount of knowledge in the world to what each of us has individually, it doesn't seem plausible that we should always be right.

You can thank confirmation bias for that comforting feeling that you are right. Confirmation bias ensures we notice the data that is consistent with our beliefs and fail to notice data that refutes them. Noticing data consistent with our beliefs not only helps us feel validated, but now we also have even more evidence that our beliefs represent truths about the world. Even though you mistakenly concluded that the driver behind you was a typical Boston driver, you take it as more evidence that you're right about Boston drivers. If someone riding with you pointed out the Kansas plate, you might defend your position by claiming he was driving someone else's car. Sometimes, we would rather reinterpret the facts than give up on our beliefs.

NOW LET'S CONSIDER how a self-reinforcing belief hardens Eli's impressions of Jeff Schaefer.

When Eli first joined the regional sales directors team and began attending staff meetings with his new peers, he paid close attention to how team members reviewed progress on their projects, answered questions from the boss, and outlined their weekly deliverables.

Jeff Schaefer always took more time speaking than any of the others. He detailed his team's accomplishments and frequently emphasized his own contributions with comments like "I focused them on the Mega Mart deal and, in the end, I was able to bring in the proposal two days ahead of the deadline," and, "There's no telling what would have happened if I hadn't intervened with James before the presentation. The rest of you guys would have looked pretty silly going into the CEO's office with last year's numbers." Jeff's progress reports have always rubbed Eli the wrong way.

Eli Rittman holds a belief that people should be humble and gracious. They should let their good work speak for itself. Eli believes that self-aggrandizing, egocentric people will never get ahead in an organization that values teamwork. Given his values and worldview, Eli is susceptible to forming a very quick negative conclusion about Jeff, whose behaviors get under his skin. Eli's confirmation bias about Jeff acts like a valve: it lets in data that corroborates what Eli believes about Jeff while shutting out data inconsistent with his preconceptions. Eli is tuned in and attentive when Jeff behaves as expected; on the other hand, Eli fails to notice any behaviors that could contradict or at least bring more balance to his conclusions about Jeff.

A few weeks after Eli joined the sales directors team, he and Molly had a meeting with Jeff and the executive VP of sales (Jeff and Eli's boss). Molly is the Pacific Northwest VP of finance and one of Eli's most trusted colleagues. Eli had come to confide in Molly and found her to be a great coach and friend.

He walked with her to the meeting that day, making it clear how much he dreaded the thought of listening to Jeff's latest accomplishments. After the meeting, Eli and Molly compared notes.

"Can you believe that guy?" Eli shook his head and then repeated one of Jeff's comments verbatim, but in a mocking tone: "My team has been singled out for a vendor award from Mega Mart."

"He can get on my nerves," Molly agreed. "On the other hand, did you see the quarterly numbers his region posted? He must be doing something right."

"I didn't bother looking at them. He's probably gaming the numbers some way." Eli went on, "How about when he dropped Frank Reinhold's name? I thought I was going to puke." Eli returned to his exaggerated Jeff imitation: "I bumped into Frank in the garage this morning and we talked for a good 20 minutes about the status of Mega Mart."

This exchange points out how the combination of confirmation bias and selective attention keeps us stuck. Eli focuses on the data from the meeting that reinforces his opinion of Jeff, while discounting and ignoring other data about the meeting that provides a more balanced picture.

Again, are you ever surprised by how often you're right? When it comes to beliefs connected to our values, we'd rather reinterpret the data than let go of a belief. "He's probably gaming the numbers some way," Eli concludes without really thinking through the accusation.

Imagine that Eli wanted and expected the promotion that went to Jeff. Let's go back to the Monday of the announcement about the promotion. Supportive, Molly gave Eli plenty of time to express his shock and anger. But even after his anger subsided, Eli felt stuck; he felt blindsided by the news of Jeff's promotion. He couldn't get past the feeling that Jeff had manipulated the situation in some way.

3 /

Our Need for Closure

We'll return to the story of Eli shortly. First, I want to continue our look at information processing errors that make it hard to get unstuck.

We've seen how confirmation bias restricts the data we notice to the data that corresponds to our worldview. Another information processing habit limits the information we consider before reaching a conclusion. It turns out that to varying degrees people show a preference for reaching conclusions quickly over continuing to process information.

Else Frenkel-Brunswik was a Polish-Austrian psychologist who left Europe for the United States in the run-up to World War II and subsequently joined the faculty at University of California–Berkeley. Earlier, her father had moved the family from Poland to Vienna in 1914 to escape the pogroms targeting Jewish families. Under the circumstances, it's not surprising that Frenkel-Brunswik became interested in the psychology of authoritarianism.

In one study, she interviewed 100 adults and 200 children, ages 9 to 14, about their attitudes toward ethnic prejudice. Her research into the origins of prejudice led to the introduction of a personality trait called *intolerance of ambiguity*. Frenkel-Brunswik linked intolerance of ambiguity to rigid, black-and-white thinking that favors certainty and familiarity.[1]

Several subsequent studies have linked intolerance of ambiguity with ethnocentrism and prejudice. In general, people who hold clear and enduring prejudices against others view differences as threatening. They have a stronger need for structure and clarity. Encountering people who don't fit the group they identify with creates stress that leads to antipathy. Having less tolerance of ambiguity often correlates with holding rigid distinctions between in-groups and out-groups.

In the late 1970s and early 1980s, studies of intolerance of ambiguity linked ambiguous situations in organizational settings (such as unclear roles) to work stress. Several scholars from diverse fields became interested in our reactions to ambiguity and uncertainty. In general, researchers concluded that—for some people and in some situations—ambiguous and uncertain conditions feel threatening. When the brain detects a threat, it responds in predictable ways.[2]

Social psychologist Arie Kruglanski built on the research into ambiguity tolerance and closed-mindedness. He and his colleagues identified a tendency to avoid the stress associated with continued processing of ambiguous information. To reduce the discomfort of continued information seeking and processing, the brain reaches a conclusion quickly and then maintains allegiance to the conclusion.

Kruglanski and his research colleagues conducted a series of experiments related to how we settle on and stick to a point of view when making decisions and solving problems. Kruglanski defined a "need for nonspecific closure" as "the individual's desire for a firm answer to a question— any firm answer as compared to confusion and/or ambiguity."[3]

In one experiment, researchers evaluated the creativity of small groups organized according to their scores on an assessment of their need for closure.[4] Participants were asked to produce advertising slogans for a product. The slogans were rated by independent judges. The researchers found that groups comprised of participants with lower need-for-closure scores demonstrated greater ideational fluency, higher degrees of elaboration, and more creativity. Another study looked into the relationship between need for closure and the desire to consult more information when forming judgments. In the study, Alain Van Hiel and Ivan Mervielde concluded that in ambiguous situations people will suspend their search for additional information and perspectives if a simple solution is available.[5] In other words, the more chaotic the environment, the more we settle for simple, definitive answers.

Often, when I read a social science study, I imagine how I would behave if I had been one of the research participants. In graduate school, I read a number of the need-for-closure studies while working on a paper about how groups make collective decisions. I consider myself an open-minded person, so I read the need-for-closure results with a certain skepticism.

Surely, I thought, I would have behaved more rationally had I been a research subject. I would never have settled for a poor-quality decision just to avoid the stress of further ambiguity.

But a few years later, after including the research on closed-mindedness in the literature review of my dissertation, I travelled to China for work and experienced firsthand the "need for closure" phenomenon.

Before the world began sheltering from the coronavirus pandemic, I travelled nearly every week for work, including dozens of trips overseas. I had previously been to China three times and felt well prepared for my visit. On previous visits, I had been greeted at the airport and transported to my hotel. On this visit, I would need to find my own way from the Beijing airport to my hotel in the Wangjing subdistrict.

Being an experienced traveler and a fairly neurotic human being, I planned meticulously. I downloaded useful apps. I printed all my destinations in Chinese characters to show taxi drivers. I made sure that my phone and credit cards would all work. Still, I felt anxious and used up a lot of mental energy imagining what might go wrong.

I landed at Beijing International, found my way to the taxi stand, and joined a long queue of people. I looked like I didn't belong, and I felt like I didn't belong (a useful experience for a white American male Baby Boomer who travelled to China to lead a workshop about adaptability). A guy approached me and in broken English explained that he would take me to my hotel. I was well aware that this was an attempt to take advantage of me, yet in my jet-lagged, anxious state of mind, I agreed. I asked about the price and he kept saying, "meter price." When we arrived at the hotel, he showed me a card with a price on it (the meter was never turned on). When I objected to the price, his English got worse and he did a lot of shrugging.

In the end, I paid 10 times the appropriate taxi fare. My driver was an opportunist who made me an offer that I would never have accepted if I hadn't been stressed out and disoriented. In a situation where nothing was making sense, I went with something that made sense; even while knowing it wasn't good for me. Applying Kruglanski's definition of need for closure, I settled for a simple, definitive answer rather than prolonged confusion and ambiguity.

We make bad decisions when we feel stress. Feeling disoriented is a particular kind of stress. I anticipated feeling disoriented because I chose to travel to a place where many of the norms I take for granted don't apply. I was prepared to feel out of place, yet I still let someone take advantage of me. Sometimes when you're worn out and worried, even a huckster can feel like a port in a storm.

In an influential 1996 publication, Kruglanski and his colleague Donna Webster described two tendencies of thought that get activated when we feel a heightened need for closure. The first is the *urgency tendency,* described as a desire to "seize" on an answer or conclusion quickly. The second is the *permanence tendency,* described as a desire to perpetuate closure or to "freeze" on an answer or conclusion so that it endures, even in the face of new, relevant information.[6]

Need-for-closure researchers have demonstrated that environmental factors can influence our seizing and freezing tendencies. They have also demonstrated through a personality assessment that some people are generally more prone to seizing and freezing than others; in other words, certain people have a greater need for closure than others. Kruglanski thinks of "closed-mindedness" as the "crystallization" of a belief occurring at the juncture in our thought process when an answer we seize on becomes a conclusion we freeze on.

I'm writing this book in the midst of arguably the most confusing, stressful, and uncertain circumstances of our lifetime. Consider how the need-for-closure research program has illuminated decision-making and problem-solving during the pandemic of 2020. We have seen leaders and others who have a high need for closure seizing on answers that feel promising and freezing on them in spite of emerging evidence invalidating premature conclusions. As the uncertainty continues, we should expect to see more snake oil—and to our surprise, we may find ourselves more inclined to buy it.

4 /

Immunity to Change

Let's get back to Eli. Before introducing his story, I mentioned two types of traps that keep us stuck. Cognitive traps, such as confirmation bias, and need for closure influence the way we process information. Other traps that keep us stuck have more to do with our emotions. Just because we are convinced that a change is a good idea (the prefrontal cortex approves), doesn't mean that we will follow through with what's needed to make the change happen.

Molly understands that Eli needs new information, but unless something changes about the way Eli thinks and feels, he'll continue to be baffled by something that at some level he's not motivated to understand, let alone change. Even if Eli comes to see that there may be more to Jeff than he was willing to look at, another feature of human psychology explains why being open to new information may not be enough to get him unstuck. If Eli is going to develop a productive working relationship with Jeff, who is now his boss, and if Eli still wants to be considered for a promotion in the future, he may need to change some habits of thought and behavior.

It's easy to change our minds about things that don't require us to change our beliefs or our worldview. A few compliments were enough to change my mind about wearing trendier blue jeans, for example, but the thought of transforming my entire wardrobe from conservative to fashion forward feels like I'm abandoning something about who I am.

The author William Bridges built a consulting practice around his theory of *transitions,* which describes the human experience of confronting change.[1] Bridges pointed out that the way we speak about change is very different from the way we experience change. We talk about change as an event with a before and an after. When actually confronting change, however, our attention is drawn to what is ending: what is going away or what we are losing. Even if the change is something we want, like a new home or a promotion at work, we grieve a little for what is being lost.

The idea that humans are more attentive to loss than to gain became a central feature of the work of Kahneman and Tversky on cognitive bias. The social scientists applied the term *loss aversion* to decision-making after research experiments repeatedly demonstrated that people prefer to avoid losses than to receive equivalent gains.

Here's a typical example of the type of questions Kahneman and Tversky were fond of asking, as described in Kahneman's 2011 book, *Thinking, Fast and Slow.* "You are offered a gamble on the toss of a coin. If the coin shows tails, you lose $100. If the coin shows heads, you win $150. Is this gamble attractive? Would you accept it?"[2]

From a purely statistical perspective, the expected value of the gamble is positive. Most people, however, reject the gamble.

"For most people, the fear of losing $100 is more intense than the hope of gaining $150," Kahneman wrote. "We concluded from many such observations that 'losses loom larger than gains' and that people are ordinarily *loss averse*."[3] He went on to claim, "Loss aversion is a powerful conservative force that favors minimal changes from the status quo in the lives of both institutions and individuals."[4]

Remember that our fictional composite Eli holds a strong worldview about humility and teamwork, and in keeping with that, he has a reputation for being conscientious and hardworking. He volunteers to help his colleagues without expecting anything in return, and no one has a better grasp of sales trends or consumer insights than Eli. During senior team presentations, everyone turns to Eli for the answer any time an executive has a question about a customer or a competitor. He also lives his humility. Eli has never been the main presenter with senior leaders or customers. In fact, he often declines to attend meetings with executives or customers if he has no specific role to play. He also avoids social events with colleagues and has made fun of sales managers who would leave work early to play a round of golf with a customer.

Now suppose that Molly suggests to Eli that he should start letting people know about his accomplishments, take the lead when presenting to senior executives, develop informal relationships with colleagues and customers, and maybe even take up golf. She might be right, but for Eli, Molly's recommendations feel scary. Eli can't focus on the potential gains he might get stepping into the spotlight and being more sociable until he has worked through his aversion to what he might be losing. Sometimes there is comfort and safety in remaining stuck.

Advances in brain imaging allow neuroscientists to observe the neural activity associated with a variety of conditions that trigger human emotions. What Kahneman and Tversky learned about loss aversion through observing people's behaviors can also be seen as patterns of activity in the brain.

A 2016 study by Jonas T. Kaplan, Sarah I. Gimbel, and Sam Harris sought to understand what happens in the brain when people holding specific political beliefs are presented with contradictory evidence. The study found that resistance to changing one's political beliefs correlated with activity in the parts of the brain associated with our reactions to threats. "One interpretation of these activations in the context of our study," they reported, "is that these structures are signaling threats to deeply held beliefs in the same way they might signal threats to physical safety."[5] In other words, there is evidence that risks to our physical well-being and risks to our social identity trigger the same self-preservation systems.

Self-preservation is how we protect ourselves from experiencing the loss associated with change. Under stress, our bodies initiate what has become known as the *fight, flight, or freeze* response. The phrase *fight, flight, or freeze* encapsulates the three options available to our prehistoric ancestors when faced with a life-threatening situation. Modern threats are different, but the stress response is the same.

On July 30, 2020, the funeral service for civil rights activist John Lewis aired on Fox News, CNN, and MSNBC. The funeral featured eulogies from former U.S. Presidents

Bill Clinton, George W. Bush, and Barack Obama. According to the Nielsen company, during the hour before the funeral Fox averaged 1.67 million viewers. During the funeral service, while viewership for CNN and MSNBC increased, Fox viewership fell to 595,000.[6] Over a million viewers fled the coverage of John Lewis's funeral! We've evolved to avoid stressful situations. We haven't evolved enough to train our stress response to recognize the difference between a life-threatening situation and opinions we don't like.

Some people avoid situations that threaten their beliefs, others impulsively lash out. In September of 2020, Donald Trump learned that the federal government had been conducting diversity and inclusion training for its employees. When segments airing on Fox News disclosed that the training programs included information about unconscious bias and "white privilege," Trump ordered the programs to stop. In a statement responding to the order, Everett Kelley, the president of the American Federation of Government Employees National said, "That the federal government is now making major policy changes based on unconfirmed press reports President Trump saw on Fox News, without even a pretense of actual research into the issue, demonstrates how far this administration has strayed from anything that remotely resembles the principles of good government."[7]

We presume that getting unstuck is like discovering a solution or an answer. Often, however, getting unstuck is less like finding a key to unlock a door and more like noticing that what we want is already in the room with us. If we are a little stuck, a nudge toward a new idea or the clearing up of a misunderstanding might just do the trick. However, if we are more desperately stuck, we won't get through it unchanged. When getting unstuck requires something personally transformative, we need to feel safe contemplating what might be ending if we were to adopt new perspectives and behaviors.

EVEN AS WE attempt to modify our worldviews, confirmation bias reassures us that our time-tested beliefs are still justified. We may suspect that some of our beliefs are holding us back, but loss aversion makes letting go of those beliefs feel unsafe. In the face of powerful conserving tendencies, how do adults, who have reached a stage of development often characterized by the stability of their worldviews, ever learn to change their minds?

One program of scholarship about how adults transform their perspectives began in 1978 with research conducted by Jack Mezirow, a pioneer of the transformative learning movement in adult education.[8] A variety of scholars and practitioners have contributed to transformative learning theory, some viewing the process as a rational coming to terms with our underlying assumptions, others viewing the process as an intuitive and holistic expansion of our consciousness.

The approaches share the idea that adults get stuck because either (a) something about the world has changed and our habits are no longer getting us what we want, or (b) something about our goals and aspirations has changed but somehow we're getting in our own way and not making progress.

Eli aspires to be seen as an influential leader ready for promotion to an executive sales role, yet his strategy for achieving his goal is to double down on what he is already known for:

being a hard-working, collaborative, yet reclusive expert on sales trends and consumer behavior.

Successful application of transformative learning always involves someone becoming aware of his or her own assumptions or frames of reference. When we are more aware of our assumptions, we can reflect critically on their validity. When we do this, we're less likely to conflate them with our identities. The transformative learning theory approach to self-reflection varies with different scholars and practitioners, but they all share the view that transformation depends on noticing and then parting company with counterproductive assumptions. Harvard professors Robert Kegan and Lisa Laskow Lahey would describe Eli as having a "competing commitment" which creates an "immunity to change."[9]

If Eli is serious about getting a promotion, he'll have to make a commitment to adopt some of the behaviors that Molly recommends. Let's say Eli agrees to seek out opportunities to share his insights and ideas about sales strategies with senior leaders. He commits to Molly that he will start speaking up in meetings, take the initiative to schedule one-on-ones with senior leaders, and tag along with sales reps when they visit customers. If Eli doesn't follow through on adopting the new behaviors, Kegan and Lahey's work suggests that Eli has something else he is committed to that competes with his stated intent to press the flesh with executives and customers. It's just that Eli is not aware of the competing commitment, or the assumptions that underlie his competing commitment.

Competing commitments protect us from experiencing emotions we most want to avoid by ensuring we get our needs met—not the needs we articulate as goals, but the hidden needs that would make us feel vulnerable if we understood and acknowledged them. Though he is largely unaware of it, Eli is committed to not being humiliated, not looking incompetent or uninformed, and he is committed to participating only when he can be recognized for his expertise. Given his hidden competing commitments, his strategies of only speaking up when he has something insightful to say and avoiding situations where he can't control the topics that might come up make perfect sense. For Eli to get unstuck, he will have to understand how his "immunity to change" operates, and he will only do so if he feels safe exploring what might be causing his behavior.

Uncovering Eli's counterproductive assumptions gets a little easier when we can engage him with compassion about what's behind his choice to contribute only when it highlights his expertise. When we can ask Eli questions and listen without judgment for his underlying beliefs and values, we may learn that Eli holds an assumption that business acumen, financial acumen, and knowing the details of consumer behavior are the most important indicators of a sales manager's competence and readiness for promotion. We may learn that Eli assumes people who build themselves up and take all the credit are compensating for their ignorance of the facts. We may learn that Eli believes you can only trust people who know their stuff.

By coming to terms with how his assumptions influence the way he feels when interacting with Jeff, Eli can learn to notice and manage his own reactions. When he learns to manage his reactions, he can make a conscious choice about how to listen and respond to Jeff. Making a conscious choice is another way of saying that Eli's prefrontal cortex is developing a strategy for managing his emotional reactions. Eli is developing his thinking stamina. With help, Eli can learn to choose actions that will further his goals when opportunities arise. Otherwise, Eli will continue to react as though something essential to his well-being is being threatened. Eli does not necessarily need to alter his underlying assumptions. It's enough that he become aware of them and the role they play in how he thinks and feels.

5 /

Organizations Can Also Be Immune to Change

Why did Blockbuster and Kodak, once undisputed leaders in their respective industries, both file for bankruptcy? You might think that each business ignored the innovations that eventually led to their downfall, but the full story is a bit more complicated.

From the vantage point of 2010, when Blockbuster declared bankruptcy, it would be easy to conclude that by the time its leaders saw the digital and streaming entertainment business coming, it was too late to transform the business. Eastman Kodak filed for Chapter 11 protection just over a year later, and rather than going out of business, its leaders decided to focus on commercial digital imaging thereafter. It would be easy to conclude that Kodak had also been blindsided by the invention of the digital camera and online photo sharing platforms.

That's not, however, what actually happened. Blockbuster turned down a chance to purchase Netflix in 2000 for $50 million (as of April 2020, Netflix was valued at $194 billion).

According to Marc Randolph, who co-founded Netflix with Reed Hastings, the CEO of Blockbuster laughed them out of the room when he heard the $50 million price tag.[1] Blockbuster wasn't caught unawares by online subscription services, it made a strategic decision to focus on its storefronts. To hedge its bets, it even developed its own online DVD subscription business in 2004.

In 1976, Kodak had an 80% market share in camera sales and a 90% market share in film and film processing. Around 2003, digital cameras began to outsell traditional film cameras. By 2006, digital cameras dominated the market.

Nevertheless, Kodak executives in the early 2000s were not asleep at the wheel. In fact, you might be surprised to learn that it was a Kodak engineer named Steven Sasson who invented the first digital camera in 1975; consequently, the Eastman Kodak Company held the first patent for digital cameras. Even more surprising, Kodak had an online photo storage and sharing platform as early as 1999. Writing for the *Harvard Business Review* in 2016, author and consultant Scott D. Anthony pointed out that Kodak created a digital camera, invested in the technology, and even understood that photos would be shared online. Where it failed was in realizing that online photo sharing *was* the new business, not just a way to expand the printing business.[2]

The leaders of Blockbuster and Kodak at the turn of this century were smart, strategic, and experienced. They understood their markets and they noticed emerging trends. They just underestimated the threat of innovation in the same way that railroad executives at the turn of 20th century disregarded the potential of the automobile.

Organizations, like individuals, suffer from biases that limit the information they consider important and misdirect what they pay attention to. Organizations, like individuals, have identities that can create immunities to change. Let's think of strategy as the product of an organization's cognitive work and culture as an organization's emotions. An organization might become stuck because of information-processing errors during strategy formation. Strategy formation errors limit what an organization pays attention to and misdirect how resources are invested. An organization might become stuck because the collective values and beliefs that define an organization's culture reflect a hidden commitment to preserving something that feels threatened by a change in strategy.

Here's a list of indicators that an organization may be clinging to a hidden commitment that keeps it stuck:

- An organization's strategy has been the same for the last several years. Each year the senior team presents a plan that looks like a slightly improved version of the status quo.
- Members of the senior team blame one another for an inability to resolve a long-standing pain point. Efforts to fix the issue have only increased resentment.
- An individual leader is unaware of the impact his or her behavior is having on others. The organization looks the other way rather than confronting the leader.
- The organization values activity. Leaders prefer reacting to taking time to thoughtfully respond. People are busy, but deep down they suspect that they are focused on the wrong priorities.

- The organization has announced a focus on innovation, collaboration, and inclusion, but leaders have not transformed the structures and mindsets in a way that will facilitate and sustain a culture change.
- The foundational assumptions of an organization's business model no longer pertain, but leaders continue to apply tried-and-true strategies in hopes that operational excellence will reinvigorate the business.

6 /

When Blind Spots and Threats Join Forces

The disciplines we'll discuss in Part Three of the book protect us from the effects of the blind spots and threats that keep us stuck. The disciplines protect our mental processes in the same way that an exercise regimen protects our health. The disciplines can also intervene when we feel stuck to provide an insight that opens up options. Before introducing the disciplines, I want to summarize the phenomena that collectively keep us and our organizations stuck. The model described below illustrates how assumptions create blind spots and how novel solutions sometimes feel threatening.

The Inquiry Loop model explains the experience of being stuck by clarifying the relationship between our worldviews and our ability to form insights that lead to new options. The figure on the next page shows how we form (and reaffirm) beliefs through the way we seek or inquire about information. The irony of the loop is that, given the way confirmation bias,

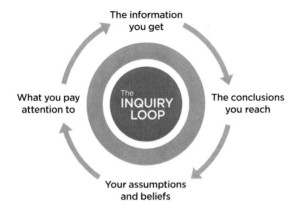

A model illustrating how our worldviews can keep us stuck if we allow blind spots to limit the information we use to reach conclusions, and if we feel threatened by conclusions that challenge our worldviews.

need for closure, loss aversion, and immunity to change team up to keep us stuck, our information-seeking strategy doesn't help us form a belief. Instead, our approach to seeking information often hardens a belief we already have. When we get stuck, beliefs aren't formed by our inquiries; rather, our inquiries simply end up preserving our beliefs.

Inquiry, in the sense used here, means more than listening or hearing. As I suggested earlier, getting unstuck means something has to change, yet our unconscious mental traps conspire against change. If you're a student or a practitioner of improvisational theater, you already know the emphasis improvisers place on the skill of listening. For the uninitiated, though, it may seem counterintuitive that actors and comedians engaged in improvisations would prioritize listening over having something interesting to say.

Keith Johnstone is a British theater director, author, playwright, and teacher who specializes in improvisational theater. Johnstone's philosophy of improvisation has a spiritual quality to it. For Johnstone, the great improvisers are channeling an emergent creation by being attentive, not by being prepared. In Johnstone's view of the art form, improvisers don't get stuck because they run out of things to say, they get stuck because they try to be clever by imposing something on a scene and then end up losing the thread of what is being created.

It's important to note that listening doesn't preclude thinking. If I'm onstage and eager to try out the Russian accent I've been practicing, I'll listen for an opportunity to introduce a character from Russia. Johnstone beautifully described what great improvisers and great listeners are listening for when he wrote, "Instead of telling actors that they should be good listeners (which is confusing), we should say, 'Be altered by what's said.'"[1] When we listen with an intention to be altered, we disrupt the stabilizing effects of the Inquiry Loop.

LET'S USE THE example of Eli to define the elements of the Inquiry Loop and how they work together to keep us stuck.

Starting at the bottom of the loop, Eli holds a set of assumptions and beliefs about Jeff. Confirmation bias orients Eli's attention to data that supports his assumptions and beliefs. Think back to how Eli ignores Jeff's accomplishments or explains his results as "gaming the numbers." As we move around the model clockwise, we now recognize that Eli doesn't seek information comprehensively. Eli seeks information based on what gets his attention, and his attention is constrained by what makes sense to his assumptions and beliefs. Eli doesn't act like a vacuum cleaner taking in everything in its path. He acts more like someone conducting an Internet search using heavily biased search terms. Think of Eli Googling "why is Jeff such a jerk?" He might get back satisfying search results, but nothing that helps him get unstuck.

Continuing around the model, we see that the conclusions Eli reaches are a direct consequence of the information he gets. Ask a bad question; get a useless answer. Remember the difference between seizing and freezing on a conclusion. Eli may have a predisposition to seek closure, and a stressful environment may make continued information processing overwhelming. Either way, Eli falls victim to need-for-closure impacts when he seizes on information about Jeff that leads to a firm and unshakable conclusion. Eli gets to feel that he's right about Jeff because he gets the information he expects to get. Seeking additional and potentially contradictory information might result in a disorienting realization.

The loop closes when Eli reaches conclusions that simply shore up his assumptions and beliefs. For Eli, an openness to new information feels risky. If he allows new information to provide a more balanced picture of Jeff, Eli might experience an emotional response not unlike the physiological response to a threat of physical harm.

Eli's worldview, bolstered by confirmation bias, restricts what Eli pays attention to. Constrained by what he pays attention to and in response to need-for-closure impacts, Eli limits his information-seeking behaviors. He seizes and freezes on a conclusion at every interaction with Jeff or whenever Jeff's name comes up in conversation. Eli's immunity to change kicks in when his conclusions confront his worldview. If adopting a revised conclusion about Jeff means losing something vital to Eli's identity, Eli will discount the conclusion and double down on his underlying beliefs and values.

In Chapter 1, we defined a problem as a situation someone wants to change. By the time Eli is faced with a situation he is motivated to change, the effects of the Inquiry Loop make change unlikely. Eli could work on changing his assumptions and beliefs so that he pays attention differently. Eli could make an effort to notice things that currently escape his attention and seek information about things he has been ignoring. But he's unlikely to. It's true that Eli went to Molly hoping for an explanation, but his inquiry was doomed by his emotional state. He didn't humbly ask Molly what he was missing about Jeff's qualifications. Instead he grumbled, "What the hell were they thinking!"

Something about Jeff irks Eli. It's not just a difference in style or priorities. For Eli, Jeff's mere presence sets off a psychological reaction not unlike an experience that triggers upsetting thoughts and emotions associated with a past trauma. If Eli can't find a productive way to cope with his reactions to Jeff, especially now that Jeff is his boss, there may come a day when an outburst from Eli derails his career.

When I first started using the story of Eli and Jeff to illustrate the conserving effects of the Inquiry Loop, I intentionally exaggerated Eli's animosity towards Jeff. Now, when I take in the current political and social landscape, Eli's diatribes against Jeff seem quaint. What started as an object lesson has become a cautionary tale.

Animosity toward those who don't share our beliefs has become a national pastime. On August 11, 2020, Marjorie Taylor Greene, a Republican politician in Georgia, won the House primary runoff election in a deeply conservative district. Green's victory is noteworthy because of her unabashed support of conspiracy theories and her documented racist, anti-Semitic, and Islamophobic statements. While high-profile Republicans like Minority Whip Steve Scalise of Louisiana have called Greene's tirades "disgusting," something else is going on here that might be even more disheartening.

Greene is betting that overwhelmed and frightened people who view diverse, progressive politicians as the enemy won't bother with her policy positions or philosophy. Greene is betting that her constituents just want someone to defeat their enemy. The game is not to demonstrate your ability to work with people who have different values in order to pass laws and improve lives. The game is to stoke animosity, hatred, and division to win an election.

Negative campaigning and divisive politics are nothing new. They always insult our intelligence and capitalize on our fears. In 1800, Thomas Jefferson ran against John Adams for President. Adam's followers referred to Jefferson as "a mean-spirited, low-lived fellow, the son of a half-breed Indian squaw, sired by a Virginia mulatto father." The Jefferson camp accused Adams of having a "hideous hermaphroditical character, which has neither the force or firmness of a man, nor the gentleness and sensibility of a woman."[2] Greene's extremism is well suited to our distressing, chaotic times. She has weaponized the blind spots and threats of the Inquiry Loop. She understands that people with a strong need for closure won't bother to learn more about her plans for governing. Greene is counting on people fearing what is different, a fear that paints political opponents as evildoers hell-bent on taking away our way of life. When we fear that something or someone threatens our way of life, our immunity to change kicks in.

As life becomes more chaotic, we take comfort in spending time with our respective tribes. Meanwhile, our ability to think and learn atrophies. Problems only get solved when something changes. When we are held captive by the Inquiry Loop, nothing changes. When our political leaders reinforce the Inquiry Loop by playing to our blind spots and exaggerating threats, government ceases to function.

More than ever, we need mental stamina to recognize and avoid the traps that keep us rooted to our ways of thinking. We don't need to safeguard our assumptions; we need to dust them off, try them on, and see if they still fit. Part Two offers an alternative to building walls around our precious belief systems.

PART TWO

THE BEGINNER'S MIND

In the beginner's mind there are many possibilities; in the expert's mind there are few.

—Shunryu Suzuki, *Zen Mind, Beginner's Mind*

7 /

Using My Useless Degree

The story goes that my parents met with my sixth-grade science teacher during a school open house. When they asked him how I was doing in class, he told them. "Well, you know what we say about Jay: often wrong, but never in doubt."

I'll never know for sure what happened during the open house because my mother always opted for the version of any event that made for the better story.

During a dinner party shortly after their visit, she shared the teacher's comment with Dora and Bernie Jacobs, friends of theirs who had known me since I was born. After hearing the story, Bernie, who disapproved of my attitude and enjoyed putting me in my place, gave me the nickname "Often."

Forty-odd years after that parent-teacher conference, I returned to school to pursue a doctorate. I remember telling Nancy Southern, the chair of my dissertation committee, the story about my parents meeting my science teacher. She seemed to enjoy the punch line a little too much. *Still?* I remember thinking, *I'm still an insufferable know-it-all?* But I'm getting ahead of myself.

After high school, I tried out several colleges and even more majors, eventually stumbling upon philosophy. I felt strangely secure there, amid the constant state of philosophical uncertainty. Come to think of it, maybe I was so committed to never being wrong that I eagerly embraced a discipline in which nobody was ever right. I loved being part of a community of people who argued in order to make ideas more beautiful and unassailable. I became a contradiction in terms, a devout doubter. I concluded that what others saw in me as a lack of doubt was to me unwillingness to accept ideas at face value.

I loved studying philosophy, but I dreaded coming home on breaks and talking to adults who wanted to ask me about school.

Dora Jacobs: "What are you studying in school?"

Me: "Philosophy."

Dora Jacobs: "What are you going to do with that?"

I would usually come up with some jokey deflection to mask my true feelings about having to defend my choice of major. "I'll open a philosophy shop," I would say. "Then I'll go into food service like everybody else with a liberal arts degree."

By the way, I did actually go into food service, although I feel like that phrase overstates the situation. I got a job washing dishes. But eventually, 20 years later, I found myself heading a corporate training and development department for Tony Roma's—a chain of casual theme restaurants—with a lot of jobs in the same industry in between. I guess you could say that food service got into me.

It's taken me years to recognize that I avoided answering the question because I felt insulted by the presumption that learning is a means to an end. Learning, like humanity in Kant's Categorical Imperative,[1] is for me an end in itself. (Hah—take that Dora Jacobs!)

In 1783, a bystander in Paris watching a hot air balloon rise into the air for the first time remarked, "But what good is it?"

"What good is a newborn baby?"[2] replied Benjamin Franklin, who was among the crowd.

When someone says they just started going to church, nobody asks what they are going to do with it. When someone confesses they've just signed up with an online dating service, nobody asks them what they are going to do with that.

Learning is my religion. Pondering the more interesting question, my constant companion.

Because I had supported myself with food service work in college, I was able to parlay my sorting skills (thoughts, silverware) into a job as a restaurant manager. For me, busyness was the antidote to paralysis caused by philosophical uncertainty. When hungry customers are lining up at the door, when servers and cooks are squabbling in the kitchen, and when bartenders are running out of clean glassware, the manager has no time to ponder the ethics of serving meat or whether alcohol influences the nature of truth.

Eventually, somebody with authority decided that I was hardworking and thoughtful and rewarded me with a promotion to the corporate office. I now had my first office job—a job that involved running around less and thinking more. A latent desire to overthink everything was no longer kept at bay by frenetic activity.

Early in my corporate career, I received a performance review warning me that I was developing a reputation for being "quodlibetic."

Seriously, my boss included the word *quodlibetic* in my performance appraisal.

According to the Merriam-Webster dictionary, the word means "consisting or of the nature of a quodlibet: purely academic; also: characterized by or fond of academic discussion."[3] I imagine my old boss wearing out a thesaurus to find a way to gently criticize me for derailing conversations with impractical questions and quibbling over inconsistencies in the way my co-workers expressed their ideas. I understood the feedback, but secretly I took it as a compliment.

Several years and a few promotions later I found myself working in an even larger corporate office for an even larger food service company. As a team leader, I was invited to attend a leadership development workshop led by a thoughtful, upbeat, and inspiring facilitator named Linda Dunkel. Linda led us through a transformative three-day workshop called Facilitative Leadership, a workshop designed by a Boston-based consulting and training firm called Interaction Associates. The moment Linda referenced Aristotle's *Rhetoric* during a lesson on how to share an inspiring vision, I knew that I would end up working for Interaction Associates.

• • •

THIS BRINGS US to the central theme of Part Two. Nearly 40 years after I earned an undergraduate degree in philosophy, and after more than 20 years as a consultant with Interaction Associates, it turns out that the world sorely needs philosophers. The world needs leaders who can access thinking tools when threats come at us from all directions.

We don't know what to do in chaotic times because we don't know how to think when things become complex and uncertain. Instead of seeking wisdom when overwhelmed, we're drawn to rash action. As a consequence, we give our attention to mindless extremists unburdened by a philosopher's obligation to make sense.

The world needs leaders and citizens with thinking skills designed for conditions of uncertainty, complexity, ambiguity, and change. I agree with the view that the global ascendency of nationalism and tribalism represent unproductive responses to people's worldview being challenged. If you yearn for the days when we considered genders as well as computational systems exclusively binary, your world has been rocking, and it shows no sign of stabilizing. It feels like everything we thought we knew is up for debate and investigation.

Philosophers are well equipped to participate in conversations about what it means to claim something is true or known. Training in philosophy prepares you to question assumptions, including your own. Unfortunately, comfort holds us back. Comfort settles for the status quo. It's reassuring to hold on to beliefs even if they no longer serve us, especially core beliefs that shape our identity. The faster things change, the more tempting it becomes to blame change rather than our capacity to adapt. Without the ability to pause for philosophically detached reflection, we not only end up with rising levels of anxiety and divisiveness, we get stuck in our thinking. Getting stuck in the way we are thinking is like finding ourselves in quicksand. The harder we struggle to find an answer, the more stuck we become.

But good news! The next two parts of this book are based upon decades of research and practice helping leaders, teams, and organizations find their way out of the quicksand. Not that it matters, but I seem to have found a way to make use of my useless degree.

8 /

Cultivating a Beginner's Mind

During the classical period of the Western world, the Greek philosopher Aristotle (469–399 BCE) catalogued the cosmos just as it appears at ground level, with the sun and moon revolving around a stationary earth. At bit later, in 270 BCE, a Greek astronomer named Aristarchus proposed a sun-centered (heliocentric) cosmology. But the general public did not accept Aristarchus's view that the earth moved around the sun. If the earth was in motion, they reasoned, we'd be able to feel it move.

When he observed that certain celestial objects (planets) did not move as predicted, Ptolemy (127–145 CE) figured out how to make the math work for the stationary earth model, at least temporarily. But ultimately science won out. History gives Copernicus (1473–1543) credit for making a heliocentric cosmology stick, dubbing the change the Copernican Revolution. Copernicus, Aristarchus, and others did not allow the certainty of appearances and mass consensus to dissuade them from considering alternatives.

Copernicus and Aristarchus exhibited a beginner's mind.

In the early 1990s, South Africa ended its decades-long policy of legally enforced racial segregation known as apartheid. President Nelson Mandela was elected in 1994 as a result, and two years later he asked Desmond Tutu to chair South Africa's Truth and Reconciliation Commission (TRC). The commission was established to investigate human rights abuses in South Africa during apartheid. An advocate of restorative justice, Archbishop Tutu proposed that the commission undertake a threefold process of confession, forgiveness, and restitution.

The TRC has been viewed by many as a model for national healing, albeit an imperfect one. In spite of calls for retribution, Mandela and Tutu believed that for the oppressed to adopt the practices of the oppressors would be a betrayal of African humanism, or *Ubuntu*. Mandela and Tutu envisioned a peaceful, thriving, multiracial nation.

Mandela and Tutu exhibited beginners' minds.

A beginner's mind is a kind of mindset. Stanford University psychologist Carol S. Dweck's 2006 bestseller, *Mindset: The New Psychology of Success*, popularized the conception of mindset as it relates to our beliefs about ourselves. Dweck made a distinction between a "fixed" mindset and a "growth" mindset. The fixed mindset operates on an assumption that our intelligence and creative capabilities are set and unchanging throughout our lives. Success to the fixed mindset is about making the most of what we've got. The growth mindset operates on an assumption that we can develop our capabilities and intelligence. For a growth mindset, success results from an unending series of improved capabilities through learning and persistence.[1]

The word *shoshin* is used in Zen Buddhism; it means, roughly, "beginner's mind." In the West, traditionally, we have made rigid distinctions between mind and body. That is less often the case in Eastern thought, and limiting shoshin to mind only does not fully capture the original Buddhist meaning. Shoshin expresses an openness of thinking, but also an open posture. It's a way of thinking *and* a way of being in the world. Whereas thinking often suggests an intentional act, shoshin is closer to what someone practicing meditation aspires to achieve.

DURING A FAMILY vacation in 1943, Edwin Land, inventor of the instant camera and co-founder of the Polaroid Corporation, took a picture of his 3-year-old daughter Jennifer with a conventional film camera of the period. He explained to Jennifer that she could see the picture after it was developed, which at the time had to be done in a darkroom or processing lab.

"Why do we have to wait?" Jennifer objected.

According to Land, Jennifer's question sparked the notion that a camera film could be invented that did not require time-consuming processing and special equipment.[2] In 1947, Land introduced the instant camera at a meeting of the Optical Society of America. A couple of years later, the camera was available to the public.

Land's daughter Jennifer demonstrated a beginner's mind by asking what some would describe as a naïve question. Naïve questions circumvent constraints and expertise because they're not burdened by assumptions about how the world works or what should or should not be done. We can all practice cultivating a beginner's mind by giving ourselves permission to admit we don't know when confronted with a question or problem. Even if we believe we know what could or should be done, we can set aside our solution temporarily and imagine the response of someone who has no expertise or experience to draw on. If you truly had no ideas, you would likely start with a question. The question would likely be naïve—and potentially as potent as Jennifer's question to her inventor dad.

The most distinctive feature of a beginner's mind is an openness to contradictions. We've seen how blind spots and threats work to limit what we notice and consider. Confirmation bias directs and restricts our attention. Need for closure shuts down our processing of information. Loss aversion and our immunity to change protect our core beliefs and assumptions from being altered by incongruous conclusions. But a beginner's mind holds assumptions and beliefs lightly, not as rigid certainties about the world. For the beginner's mind, adopting assumptions and beliefs is more like renting to buy than like making a purchase. Consequently, opinions and information that contradict don't get filtered out; instead they are welcomed and given full consideration.

Roger Martin is a professor emeritus at the Rotman School of Management at the University of Toronto. Martin served as the school's dean from 1998 to 2013. Martin has written several books on business concepts, including the concept of integrative thinking. For Martin, an integrative thinker can "hold two conflicting ideas in constructive, almost dialectic tension."[3] Martin describes integrative thinkers as having an "opposable mind." He likens the productive tension applied by an opposable mind to the productive tension created by our opposable thumbs.

He also points out that we often prefer to reduce the complexity of opposing ideas by favoring one and thereby rejecting the other. "We often don't know what to do with fundamentally opposing models. Our first impulse is usually to determine which is 'right' and, by process of elimination, which is "wrong."[4] The beginner's mind is an opposable mind.

The novelist F. Scott Fitzgerald was observing the same phenomenon when he wrote, "The test of a first-rate intelligence is the ability to hold two opposed ideas at the same time and still retain the ability to function."[5]

A mind can get stuck by being rooted in certainty. A mind can also get stuck in debilitating doubt or unproductive spinning. While the beginner's mind is open to change, it doesn't resist trying out a point of view. Consistent with a growth mindset, the beginner's mind values learning. Learning helps the beginner's mind access a variety of ideas, make reference to diverse expertise, and notice patterns. The beginner's mind draws on what it has learned and then experiments with an assumption that operates like a working theory. If the experiment fails, the beginner's mind racks up another useful lesson.

When working with clients who seek to develop their leaders' strategic agility, I start from the premise that strategic agility benefits from a beginner's mind. After all, being strategic means having a plan. Being agile means being able to make quick and easy movements. Putting them together means having enough certainty to choose a destination while simultaneously being attentive to signals that present viable alternatives and breakthrough options.

The Lego Group, makers of the interlocking plastic bricks beloved by children and cursed by barefoot parents across the globe, has demonstrated decades of strategic agility. In 2005, the company was losing money; by 2012 the Lego Group surpassed Mattel to become the world's most valuable toy company. To date, Lego has managed to experiment and innovate with moves into entertainment, theme parks, retail, and digital. At the same time, Lego is guided by its brand framework that envisions the company as a "global force for establishing and innovating Learning-through-Play."[6]

Without a strategy, interesting ideas and trends become distracting shiny objects. Without agility, anomalies that signify you're heading in the wrong direction get overlooked. Aristarchus and Copernicus didn't try to fit their observations into the prevailing worldview; they wondered if the anomalies they observed might be clues to a new paradigm. Mandela and Tutu empathized with growing demands for vengeance but held fast to a strategy based on core principles. The beginner's mind holds the tension between strategy and agility while applying the four disciplines we will meet later to consciously choose a path forward.

HUMANS LIKE TO categorize things; some researchers believe that it's part of our nature.[7] We don't see a rainbow as the spectrum of light, which it is. We perceive a rainbow as an arc of distinct bands of color. As we learn more about our planet's living things, we discover organisms that stubbornly defy the standard classification system originated by Carl Linnaeus in 1758. Yet, rather than abandoning the notion of a taxonomy, biologists keep tweaking it.[8]

For most of my life, gender fell into two categories, male and female. At last count, Facebook has 71 gender options to choose from, and it recently added a free-form field if you don't identify with any of the options provided. The instinct to add a new category when something doesn't fit reflects our fondness—maybe our need—for understanding the world by comparing and contrasting.

As I write this chapter, even the wearing of face coverings to slow the spread of Covid-19 places people into categories— categories imbued with political overtones. A May 2020 Politico article had this headline: "Wearing a mask is for smug liberals. Refusing to is for reckless Republicans."[9]

The beginner's mind builds categories too. The difference is the attitude about what the category represents. Patterns, themes, and other similarities can provide helpful ways to understand the nature of a situation so that we can choose appropriate options when we want to make a change. Categories, to the beginner's mind, are useful constructs only until they stop being useful. An anomaly or outlier is something that doesn't fit an established category. The stuck mind dismisses the anomaly in favor of the category. The beginner's mind wonders what possibilities the anomaly represents.

The beginner's mind entertains categories, including conflicting categories. The beginner's mind also constructs continua, when categories create limitations. For example, when gender identities and sexual orientation no longer conform to traditional categorization, the beginner's mind lets go of the categories and thinks about ranges. In another example, in 2003, when the Human Genome Project was complete, researchers imagined that they would be able to connect a diagnosis of autism to specific genes. Instead, they found that hundreds of genes were involved, but none linked exclusively to autism. In response, rather than create a taxonomy of autism, clinicians have chosen to describe a range of autism characteristics from mild to severe.[10] We now think of people as being "on the spectrum," rather than being stuck with the unhelpful binary choice of "having" or "not having" a particular type of autism.

The beginner's mindset is grounded in bedrock values. The beginner's mind trusts that learning is its own reward. The beginner's mind presumes that, as humans, we have the agency and capacity to determine our futures and solve our problems. The beginner's mind accepts responsibility for the greater good by prioritizing fulfillment and development over material gain or personal comfort.

We have seen that the key feature of a beginner's mind is the ability to comfortably entertain conflicting ideas, to inhabit the space between opposing perspectives without feeling the need to choose sides. The calling to be both principled and tolerant creates just such tensions. Rather than explore the topic conceptually, let's consider a real-world example that challenges us to find a way forward when tolerance and principled action collide.

In April of 2011, France became the first European country to impose a ban on full-face coverings such as the niqab and the burka. The niqab and the burka are both worn by some Muslim women, in observance of some, but not all, interpretations of Islamic law. In 2018, the United Nations Human Rights Committee declared that France's ban represents a violation of human rights. Let's set aside the related issue a libertarian might raise about whether or not it's appropriate for a government to decide what can and cannot be worn. What position do you take on the issue of women wearing full-face veils in public?

The point of the thought experiment is not to debate answers. The point of the thought experiment is to experience the tension of weighing options that raise competing interests. If answering the question is easy for you, you are likely applying a certainty born of values and beliefs that you have consciously adopted or have been raised to accept. If answering the question feels hard, if you keep layering on factors and considerations, you are developing your beginner's mind. (By the way, in an interesting plot twist, France has mandated face masks to control the spread of the coronavirus but continues its ban on burkas and niqabs.[11])

The beginner's mind is not paralyzed by juggling variables and possibilities. The beginner's mind is inspired and energized by alternatives. The beginner's mind develops insights and options by sitting with, rather than avoiding, questions and tensions. Getting comfortable with questions and tensions makes the space between certainty and uncertainty more habitable.

9 /

Question-ability

The customary use of *questionability* comes with negative connotations. Dictionaries link questionability to the state of being questionable, or dubious. If, for example, people refer to the questionability of your character, they're not suggesting that your character deserves further investigation; they mean you aren't to be trusted.

We're going to destigmatize *questionability* by focusing on its two stem words: *question* and *ability*. For our purposes, *question-ability* means the ability to question, to use our mental capacity to improve our questions when we're stuck for an answer. To develop a beginner's mind, start with developing your ability to ask better questions.

People with question-ability are naturally curious and ask a lot of questions. Einstein famously advised that "the important thing is to never stop questioning. Curiosity has its own reason for existing."[1]

People with question-able intelligence not only ask a lot of questions; they are also skilled at improving their questions when they're stuck for an answer. Question-able people recognize when the questions under consideration unintentionally limit, misdirect, or exclude.

A well-known story about improving a question involves the owner of a high-rise office building. The source of the story is unknown, but a detailed treatment of the story can be found in Thomas Wedell-Wedellsborg's 2020 book, *What's Your Problem?*

The story goes that tenants working in the office building have been complaining that the elevators take too long to arrive after they push the up or down button.

The owner first considers the question of how to speed up the elevators. Improving the performance of the elevators would likely involve expensive equipment upgrades and time-consuming renovation. Displaying a high degree of question-ability, the owner then considers the question of how to help his tenants feel less bored while waiting for the elevators to arrive.[2] Focusing on making the wait less annoying does not preclude equipment upgrades, but it also allows for others options like mirrors, or screens displaying news. The reframed question is also better because it's centered on the people who experience a dissatisfying situation.

There was a time when people thought the earth was flat—apparently some still do. When you think of the earth as flat, it's reasonable to ask what lies beyond the edge of the world. Leaps of progress don't arise from answering the wrong questions. Real progress results from changing our questions.

As questions improve, inadequate answers lose their footing, which clears the way for even better questions.

Questions are powerful to the degree they are subversive. The ancient Greek philosopher Socrates developed a reputation as a relentless questioner. As described in the works of his student Plato, Socrates would begin conversations with a question about the nature of a concept: What is justice? What is love? What is truth? The Socratic method of teaching continues to be used because of its value in developing critical thinking. Sadly, questions that spur critical thinking are not always welcomed by those in authority. Socrates was eventually charged with corrupting the youth of Athens, imprisoned, and sentenced to death.

Hal Gregersen is the executive director of the MIT Leadership Center. He also teaches courses on leadership and innovation at the MIT Sloan School of Management. In his 2018 book, *Questions Are the Answer: A Breakthrough Approach to Your Most Vexing Problems at Work and in Life*, Gregersen wrote:

> My contention is that this is how a great deal of progress happens. Questions are reframed in ways that prove catalytic. They dissolve barriers to thinking, like limiting prior assumptions, and they channel creative energy down more productive pathways. People who have been feeling stuck suddenly see new possibilities and are motivated to pursue them.[3]

I am making a similar claim. Whether you're stuck trying to understand something complex or you're stuck trying to meet a practical need, the key to making progress may be hidden in the questions you are asking. The key to getting unstuck is to boost your question-ability.

Ron Heifetz and Marty Linsky are professors at Harvard's Kennedy School of Government and co-founders of the firm Cambridge Leadership Associates. In many of their articles and books about leadership, Heifetz and Linsky describe the challenge of gaining perspective in the midst of action as metaphorically "getting on the balcony" as opposed to "being on the dance floor."[4]

Leaders get things done through interactions on the dance floor, but it's difficult to grasp the big picture while moving among a crowd of dancers. Heifetz and Linsky suggest that leaders learn to adapt by occasionally leaving the dance floor and taking in the view from the balcony. From the balcony, leaders notice how people are moving and how they react when the music changes. The leader on the balcony can think strategically and develop a plan. The balcony offers a useful view, but the leader cannot influence the action from the balcony. Having developed a plan informed by the balcony perspective, the leader can return to the dance floor. The leader may now choose to dance in a new way, dance with new partners, or perhaps suggest a change of music.

Question-ability is about "getting on the balcony" with respect to the questions we ask about situations we want to change. We rarely pause to consider how the questions we pose commit us to an unproductive way of thinking or acting. When we hear a question, we instinctively want to offer our thoughts, opinions, conclusions, and solutions.

Remember the picture of my daughters' bathroom from Chapter 1? I often show a slide of the image when I lead workshops on strategic agility. While the group looks at the picture, I ask, "How do I get my daughter to keep her bathroom clean and organized?" and then pause to take in the advice. I hear answers like, "Get a trash bag," or "Close the door," or "Have a conversation with your daughter about respect."

On rare occasions, a workshop participant will answer my question with a question, such as, "Why do you want to do anything about this?" or "How does your daughter feel about the condition of the bathroom?" Questions that present a pause in the action to investigate how I'm thinking about my situation represent a different category of response from a simple answer or suggestion.

To extend (perhaps overextend) Heifetz and Linsky's metaphor, answering my question is dancing with me. Questioning my question represents an invitation to the balcony. On the dance floor we consider how to make a change. On the balcony we consider how to define the situation we want to change. People with question-able intelligence want to explore whether the question itself, rather than the lack of an answer, may be the barrier to getting unstuck.

A word of warning. Question-ability without being emotionally attuned to other people can make you annoying and unpopular. In the case of Socrates, it meant jail and a death sentence. Recall the story in Chapter 7 about my early corporate experiences. I developed a reputation for derailing conversations in meetings by posing questions that people considered impractical. I ended up being excluded from the planning and problem-solving discussions that I enjoy. On the plus side, I got invited to a lot fewer meetings.

I still spend too much time on the balcony questioning people's questions. Fortunately, I now have a business partner who drags me onto the dance floor to get things done. Lisa will tolerate the questions, but not at the expense of progress and momentum.

IF YOUR ORGANIZATION promotes leaders to roles of greater authority and responsibility based exclusively on their experience and knowledge, you shouldn't be surprised when they apply tried-and-true approaches in their new role. Leaders who rely on detailed expertise about operating the business tend to micromanage and have difficulty adapting to environmental changes. Making knowledge and experience top criteria for promotion into an organizational leadership role only makes sense if the basic operating assumptions of the business and the fundamentals of the marketplace remain unchanged.

In 1993, IBM hired Louis V. Gerstner Jr. as CEO. IBM had not hired a CEO from outside the company since 1914. The company's dominance in the technology sector had eroded with the rise of the personal computer and the introduction of the client-server model, which provided an alternative to IBM's bread and butter, the mainframe computer. From the beginning of the 1980s to the end of the decade, IBM's revenues dropped by $2 billion. In its 1992 fiscal year, IBM posted a $8.1 billion loss.

Gerstner didn't arrive at IBM with answers; he arrived with questions. He'd previously been CEO of RJR Nabisco, and before that president of American Express, so he didn't know a lot about IBM's business going in. He spent his first 30 days listening and questioning. Because he didn't have an emotional attachment to IBM's existing business model, products, or culture, Gerstner applied his question-able intelligence to listening for the assumptions that were keeping IBM stuck. Gerstner shepherded a number of transformational changes at IBM, many of which came from radical ideas within the company that had not been taken seriously. By 1994, IBM was in the black, posting a $3 billion profit.[5]

Ninety percent of IBM's profit in 1993 came from the sale of mainframe computers. In his first days with the company, he met with the mainframe team and learned of rapidly declining sales and a falloff in market share. He was told that Hitachi, Fujitsu, and Amdahl were pricing mainframes 30% to 40% below IBM.

Like Edwin Land's daughter, Gerstner asked a beginner's question: "Why don't we lower our prices?"

The mainframe team explained that lowering prices would cause a substantial loss at a time when IBM badly needed profits. It became clear to Gerstner that IBM was milking the profits from an important product while betting that customers would simply put up with higher prices. Gerstner had also listened to IBM's customers, who were pleading with IBM to offer competitive pricing so they wouldn't have to endure the pain of switching out their computer systems.

He told the mainframe team to come up with an aggressive price reduction plan that he could announce at a major customer conference happening in two weeks.[6]

Gerstner's question-ability exposed previously unquestioned assumptions at IBM. Question-ability also allows leaders to find hidden gems in ideas that don't initially appear promising.

When knowledgeable leaders hear a new idea, they consider the feasibility and viability of the idea in light of their experience. When question-able leaders hear a new idea, they get curious about where the idea came from and what the idea allows for.

Here's a quick experiment you can try the next time someone suggests an idea that strikes you as useless or counterproductive. Instead of explaining why it won't work, ask the person with the idea this question: What brought that idea to mind?

How you ask, of course, is as important as what you ask. Your question should not come across as a rebuke of the form: What were you thinking?!

If you can muster authentic curiosity and inquire into the thinking behind what seems like a lousy idea, you may find yourself in a generative conversation that opens things up rather than shuts things down.

IF OUR FUTURE depends on leaders who can be effective under conditions of uncertainty and complexity, maybe it's time we deemphasize knowing and expertise in favor of discovering and inquisitiveness. Question-ability is a job requirement for philosophers, scientists, and journalists—why not leaders? Maybe we need an award for the year's most question-able leader, an award you'd be honored to receive.

Question-able intelligence also comes in handy when we're overwhelmed by the amount of information coming at us. Without the ability to question what we read, hear, and watch, we settle for the information that's most easily digested, whether or not it's accurate or relevant. To be more question-able is to be a more discerning consumer of information.

Think back to the discussion of the Inquiry Loop in Chapter 6. Our blind spots and our responses to anything that threatens our worldview make it difficult for us to change our minds. Without the ability to take a "balcony" perspective on our own thinking, we become more hostile to opinions that don't align with our worldview.

In 2017, the Pew Research Center published a study of partisanship in the United States.[7] It has been conducting the same survey since 1994. The survey collects opinions on issues like the role of government, the environment, race, and immigration. In 1994, the gap in responses across 10 such topics between Democrats and Republicans was 15 percentage points. In 2017 the gap between Democrats and Republicans had risen to 36 percentage points. In his 2020 book *Why We're Polarized*, the political analyst and co-founder of Vox News Ezra Klein summed up the Pew study:

It's worth being clear about what this means: if you're a Democrat, the Republican Party of 2017 poses a much sharper threat to your vision of a good society than the Republican Party of 1994 did. It includes fewer people who agree with you, and it has united around an agenda much further away from yours. The same is true, of course, for Republicans peering at the modern Democratic Party.[8]

Question-able people are naturally curious and analytical. To be question-able is to treat each claim made by another person as an artifact rather than an objective fact. Artifacts, like opinions, are constructed by humans. Question-able people want to know sources. They want to understand what motivates a person to express themselves in a particular way. Question-able people favor learning over knowing, because a preference for learning equips us to adapt to a changing world, whereas a preference for knowing motivates us to keep things as they are.

Question-able leaders are skilled at improving their questions when they're stuck for an answer. Question-able citizens seek to liberate themselves from the thinking traps that isolate and divide us.

10 /

The Downside of Expertise

In August of 2019, I developed a rash that defied various over-the-counter treatments and web-sourced home remedies. The first dermatologist I saw ordered a skin biopsy and then fixated on something called a drug eruption, based on the lab report. As the name suggests, a drug eruption is caused by a reaction to medication. I was advised to eliminate my daily cholesterol medicine and any other over-the-counter drugs I might take for aches and pains.

Months went by, during which I would experience intermittent relief followed by a return of the symptoms. After complaining to my family physician, he referred me to a different specialist. The new dermatologist took one look at me, put some scrapings under a microscope, and told me I had scabies. After two treatments spaced a week apart, I was cured.

Scabies is a revolting condition; I'll spare you a description. Ask Siri or Alexa if you must, but don't say I didn't warn you. The second dermatologist, to whom I will be forever grateful, explained that I don't look like someone you would expect to have scabies, and my profession and routines were very unlikely to have exposed me to scabies. He wasn't surprised that the first dermatologist missed it. It's worth noting that the second dermatologist had one important advantage over the first dermatologist. The second dermatologist was not attached to the drug eruption hypothesis.

The more you know about a subject, the more difficult it is for you to ask questions that illicit new insights. When experts frame questions, their questions become infested (so to speak) by their experiences and worldviews. Most experts can't help forming quick hypotheses about a situation when they encounter information connected to their previous experience. When experience is upended by new realities or new possibilities, expertise can become a liability. The tricky part is recognizing when your expertise is getting in the way (as in the case of the first dermatologist) and when your expertise should be trusted (as in the case of the second dermatologist).

One of my favorite passages from Lewis Carroll's *Alice in Wonderland*, is his description of the Queen of Heart's croquet match:

Alice thought she had never seen such a curious croquet-ground in her life; it was all ridges and furrows; the croquet-balls were live hedgehogs, and the mallets live flamingoes, and the soldiers had to double themselves up and stand on their hands and feet, to make the arches. The players all played at once without waiting for turns, quarrelling all the while, and fighting for the hedgehogs; and in a very short time the Queen was in a furious passion, and went stamping about, and shouting, "Off with his head!" or "Off with her head!" about once in a minute.[1]

Carroll captures the disorienting feeling of engaging in a familiar activity only to discover that the rules of play keep changing. As conditions change, we need to reevaluate our typical responses. When conditions become unpredictable, the capacity to learn, improvise, and adapt become more important than making choices based on our previous experience.

There is an acronym for such perplexing and fickle conditions: VUCA. The term has been used by the U.S. Army War College since the early 1990s to describe dynamic battlefield conditions characterized by volatility, uncertainty, complexity, and ambiguity.

In a VUCA environment we experience the volatility of constant change, the uncertainty of finding ourselves in unfamiliar situations, the complexity associated with having to consider a large number of variables, and a state of ambiguity in which conditions can be interpreted in multiple and sometimes contradictory ways.

As I write this chapter, it's the spring of 2020 and I'm sheltering in my home in compliance with Dallas County guidelines implemented the week before in an effort to slow the spread of the Covid-19 virus. I can't think of a better example of VUCA conditions than the pandemic currently challenging local and national leaders around the globe—not to mention the rest of us.

The pandemic has turned the conversation about expertise from a philosophical exploration into an urgent debate about what advice to trust. Two types of expertise are on display as we grapple with real-world dilemmas such as how to contain the spread of the virus or what to do about reopening schools. The first type of expert has a beginner's mind and might be called a *learner*. We'll refer to the second type of expert who has a fixed mind as a *know-it-all*. Since I consider myself a reformed know-it-all, let me offer a defense of listening to learners in times of uncertainty.

Before we reach high school, we learn about the scientific method. In its simplest form, the scientific method starts when a question about an observation leads us to form a testable hypothesis. We run experiments based on what our hypothesis predicts and then learn from the results. If you accept the idea that we should learn from the results, you must also accept the idea that your hypothesis might be mistaken. The know-it-all prizes being right over learning something new, so we shouldn't be shocked when a know-it-all disregards the scientific method.

Under VUCA conditions, we should be skeptical of anyone claiming to be an expert, especially if their expertise is based on conditions that no longer exist. Unfortunately, when chaos ensues, we lack the thinking stamina to break free of the Inquiry Loop, and we may be inclined to put our trust in simplistic answers from people we identify with.

Under VUCA conditions, I choose to put my trust in an expert who is a learner, not a know-it-all. In the early days of the Covid-19 outbreak, Dr. Anthony Fauci, a physician, immunologist, and head of the National Institute of Allergy and Infectious Diseases, advised the public not to wear face coverings. Dr. Fauci wasn't the only expert discouraging face masks in March of 2020. The U.S. Surgeon General, Dr. Jerome Adams, as well as the Centers for Disease Control and the World Health Organization, all concluded that face coverings were unnecessary for the general public and that their use might inadvertently limit supplies for emergency workers and hospital staff.[2]

By April, however, researchers had learned that the new coronavirus spread more easily than previously believed. They discovered that asymptomatic people can spread the virus. They conducted experiments to test how long droplets remain in the air when someone who is infected is talking and breathing. In light of what the scientists learned, Dr. Fauci, Dr. Adams, the CDC, and the WHO, reversed their guidance on wearing masks.

Donald Trump took the reversal as a sign that Dr. Fauci is not trustworthy. I took it as a sign that even a leading expert on infectious diseases understands the importance of testing hypotheses and revising faulty assumptions under volatile conditions. The social philosopher Eric Hoffer summed it up well: "In times of drastic change, it is the learners who inherit the future. The learned will find themselves beautifully equipped to live in a world that no longer exists."[3]

We feel comfortable with leaders who have experience and expertise, but it's difficult for an expert to approach a problem with a beginner's mind. It's especially difficult when the problem looks familiar to the leader. Over the last several years, I have been collecting the questions organizational leaders ask about challenging situations. I've seen how the questions people ask about the situations they want to change reveal a lot about how they are thinking. One can learn to see thinking and feeling traps by paying attention to the form of the question.

I refer to questions prompted by our blind spots and threat responses as *quicksand questions*. With quicksand questions, the more we focus on answering the question, the more stuck we become. Think back again to the example from Chapter 1 of my reaction to my daughters' bathroom. The question of how to get Hannah to keep her bathroom clean and organized is a quicksand question prompted by what I'd chosen to focus on, plus an emotional response connected to my values. When generating solutions based on the initial framing of a quicksand question, things are likely to get worse, not better.

To make the idea of questioning our questions more practical, I have identified four categories of quicksand questions. If your initial framing of a question about a situation that has you stuck falls into one or more of the four categories, there's a good chance that you won't see new options until you change the question.

TYPES OF QUICKSAND QUESTIONS

Questions that impose conclusions

The mythology that leaders must have a point of view about any and all situations persists. Whether or not leaders have a strong point of view about a situation, they definitely have a bias for action. We shouldn't be surprised that, when feeling stuck or challenged by a complex situation, leaders quickly form conclusions and then set about making changes consistent with their conclusions. The urge to fix things frequently shows up in the way we pose a question about a situation we want to change.

For example, when confronted with complaints that support functions (human resources, legal, IT) felt left out and underutilized, one leader I worked with described his challenge this way: "How do we improve communication between line leaders and their support functions?"

A careful look at the question reveals a point of view about how to respond to complaints about feeling left out and underutilized. The question also implies a call to action. The leader sees the solution as improved communication and seeks help implementing a fix that might include behavior change, education, or perhaps a new knowledge management tool.

As it turned out, a lack of communication was merely a symptom of a more systemic problem. Many of the line leaders felt overly regulated when they involved support functions in their planning processes. The line leaders worked around their support functions to get things done faster. The support functions pointed out that the rush to action often meant that they had to do damage control later, but the line leaders concluded that cleaning up a small mess was preferable to missing a deadline or being unable to jump on an opportunity.

Either/or questions

Either/or questions set up a false dichotomy or false choice. The question gets framed (sometimes intentionally) to limit answers to one of two opposing options.

In reality, options are rarely, if ever, mutually exclusive. False dichotomies have rhetorical impact, but almost always contain a logical fallacy. You can easily imagine a politician declaring a choice between voting in favor of a piece of legislation or condemning the country to a future of lawless anarchy.

Here's a false dichotomy question that lured a leader into posing a different kind of quicksand question: Should we bring in someone from outside the company to head up the marketing department or promote someone from within?

In fact, there are other alternatives. For example, they might hire someone from the outside as a chief of staff to support and mentor an internal hire that runs the department.

Questions about getting others to change

Sometimes, when we feel stuck and can't control all the variables influencing our dissatisfying situation, we assign blame: If only our suppliers would lower their prices. If only our employees would act with greater accountability. If only our salespeople would forecast the pipeline more accurately.

You could argue that the get-others-to-change framing is a special case of the questions-that-impose-conclusions framing. The stuck leader in this category of quicksand question has concluded that the identified group or individual must change their behavior for the organization to make progress.

In my experience, organizational leaders pose questions about getting others to change so often that the get-others-to-change framing deserves its own category.

I worked with a leader in an insurance company who had been assigned the goal of increasing sales of bundled insurance products. (Bundling insurance simply means putting together more than one insurance product—car insurance, home insurance, life insurance—from the same company.) The leader had initiated a number of projects with the task of finding answers to the question of how to get the company's agents to cross-sell its products. The projects were unsuccessful.

When we accept a get-others-to-change framing of a dilemma, we end up thinking of people as automatons. Solving our problem becomes an exercise in figuring out the programming required to alter the behaviors we find troublesome or installing new behaviors to produce the outcomes we want (say, for example, programming a daughter to keep her bathroom tidy).

In the case of the insurance company, a few questions about its agents unlocked a new approach. The leader explained that people who make the best agents see themselves as leaders in their communities. They get involved and make a point of knowing their neighbors. Successful agents want to help community members make smart choices about protecting their families and their property.

After talking it over for a few minutes, we developed a new question. Instead of thinking about *getting* agents to cross-sell insurance products, we framed a different challenge: How might we *help* our agents become the most trusted resource in their community for information about the risks of loss, injury, and damage?

It should be clear from contrasting the questions that answering the initial question would generate very different solutions than answering the reframed question. Getting unstuck means having new and interesting options.

Improperly scoped questions

The scope of a question can be too narrow or too broad. When we experience a problem in a specific way, we may arbitrarily narrow our focus. I've worked with a number of human resources leaders who have been asked to respond to disturbing trends in their employee engagement surveys. Let's say a survey shows a decline in scores related to trust in leadership. We could be limiting ourselves by asking a too-narrow question: How do we improve the trust scores on our engagement survey? Alternatively, we could err in the other direction by asking an overly broad question: How do we improve trust around here? The first question focuses our attention on the survey rather than the purpose of the survey. The second question gives us no place to start.

THE TABLE ON the following page displays several examples from individuals and groups I have worked with over the last few years who felt stuck. In the second column, I've listed the quicksand question that started the conversation about a situation worth changing. In the third column, I've listed the reframed challenge in the form of a better question.

SAMPLE QUICKSAND QUESTIONS REFRAMED

Client / Context	Quicksand Question	Reframed Question
My wife and I after encountering our daughters' bathroom	How do we get Hannah to keep her bathroom clean and organized?	How do we reduce the amount of nagging at home?
Insurance company leader who wants to increase the sale of bundled insurance products	How do we get our agents to cross-sell our insurance products?	How might we help our agents become the most trusted resource in their community for information about the risks of loss, injury, and damage?
An HR business partner supporting the finance organization trying to get senior finance leaders to coach and mentor their successors	How do we get finance leaders to give and receive feedback?	How do we help emerging finance leaders get the support they need for career growth?
A business roundtable of senior talent development professionals imagining new approaches to succession planning	How do we accelerate readiness for key roles in our organization?	How might we design organizations that are less dependent on the skills and experiences of individuals?
The leader of a software development group within a global tech company frustrated by constant requirement changes	How do stop firefighting and stick to a plan?	How might we better predict customer needs and priorities?
A state medical society task force chartered by the governor to recommend regulations to reduce opioid addiction	How do we get health plans to pay for massage and acupuncture?	How might we make it easier for people suffering from chronic pain to explore and access alternative therapies?
The director of intern programs for one business unit of a Fortune 500 consumer packaged goods company	How do we standardize our intern programs?	How might we help our most promising interns develop stronger working relationships with hiring managers?
A newly promoted senior director preparing to meet with the chief marketing officer about the new job	What are my new responsibilities?	How would you describe the value I bring to our customers in this new role?

Contrast the quicksand questions in the table with the reframed questions. What feels different about the reframed questions? What do the questions in the third column have in common? Imagine that you were one of the people at the heart of each issue. How would you feel about participating in a conversation framed by the quicksand questions versus the reframed question?

The Inquiry Loop explains how our thinking gets smaller until we're stuck in a pattern of thought. Our worldview narrows our focus. Our narrowed focus constrains our openness to unexpected or conflicting information. We end up framing our challenge as a quicksand question because of a bias for closure and a bias for action. The answers we get by asking a quicksand question are the answers we already expect, which leaves us with conclusions that support and reinforce our worldviews—and around we go. The reframed questions in the table essentially shift the description of the situation we want to change by enlarging our thinking.

For example, suppose you were my daughter Hannah, and I announced to you on your way to school in the morning that over dinner we would be discussing how to get you to keep your bathroom clean and organized. Now instead, suppose I told you that over dinner we would be discussing ways to reduce the amount of nagging going on at home. I get that for most teenagers neither conversation is appealing. But at least the one about reducing nagging stands a better chance of addressing a situation we are all motivated to change.

People with expertise and experience ask useful questions. Sometimes, however, we want more from a question than usefulness. Sometimes we want a transformational insight or a novel possibility. When conditions change, a formerly helpful question can turn counterproductive. At the current moment, crowding people into airplanes during a pandemic is not safe. Airline companies have more important questions to ponder than figuring out how to cram more people onto each flight. One telltale sign that expertise has stopped being helpful is when a seemingly useful question fails to spark answers that make a positive difference.

When your expertise kicks in, you might get fixated on an ineffectual answer. If your situation isn't improved by applying your expertise, first embrace a beginner's mind by jettisoning assumptions, and then find a better question to ask about the situation you want to change.

11 /

Thinking How to Think

People who feel overwhelmed, confused, stressed out, or stuck want to know what to do. If you can find a useful answer that provides relief, all is well. If, however, the situation doesn't improve or the problem returns after a brief improvement, you're likely to feel even worse, maybe even defeated. Sometimes the situation feels incomprehensible, and no one has a useful idea about what to do.

The mission of this book is to provide an alternative to the quest for something to do. When you don't know what to do, seeking an answer may not be the only available strategy. You might also try seeking a different question.

With the possible exception of ethicists, philosophers aren't in the business of telling people what to do. Philosophers are concerned with what things mean and why we think the way we do. Don't call a philosopher when a situation calls for swift action. On the other hand, they are uniquely qualified to help sort things out when the territory is chaotic, baffling, or uncharted. Philosophers don't just know how to think, they know how to think about how to think.

The chaos, instability, and turbulence we're currently experiencing calls for a particular type of thinking. In truth, our world was becoming more complex and uncertain long before 2020. It's worth considering whether our lack of stamina for thinking, our attraction to simplistic answers, and our shrinking attention spans are the causes rather than the results of our interlocking crises. Either way, our future may depend on the kind of unfettered thinking characteristic of a beginner's mind rather than the dog-eared playbook of incurious experts.

If those responsible for your early development didn't nurture the beginner's mind that we all start off with, I have good news. It's not too late. Learning to ask better questions—enhancing your question-ability—will help you resist the limitations of the Inquiry Loop. Training yourself to ask better questions is a practical thinking regimen for developing a beginner's mind. Questions will help build your stamina for ambiguity, complexity, and uncertainty.

In Part Three we will explore four ways to find better questions, questions that will lead to new insights and options when things feel complex and uncertain. If you are just starting to exercise your question-ability, you may be tempted to ask what makes one question better than another. That's a good question!

Before we invest time and energy answering a reframed question, we want some assurance that it will liberate us from the quicksand of the wrong question. While a better question is no guarantee of a better answer, there are four important characteristics that will indicate that your reframed question will help you get unstuck. I'll illustrate each characteristic using the messy bathroom situation.

CHARACTERISTICS OF PROPERLY REFRAMED QUESTIONS

The question helps you reduce the risk of missing something important

If my wife and I focus our attention on keeping the bathroom tidy, we miss the opportunity to have a more important conversation about respect and shared responsibility. When we switch the definition of the problematic situation from *too much clutter* to *too much arguing,* we open up the discussion to include relationship issues that are more important than messiness.

The question helps you avoid solving the wrong problem

Is it really about the way the bathroom looks? When we think about getting Hannah to keep the bathroom tidy, we conclude that Hannah, her attitude, and habits are the problem. You know you've solved the wrong problem if the problem comes back. Hannah might comply with our demands and clean up the bathroom. Later, when she leaves her dirty clothes on the floor, we might once again become argumentative. When we think about reducing the amount of nagging at home, we accept that we all have a part in creating a situation that we want to change.

The question helps you discover previously excluded perspectives

It's natural for someone who feels stuck to frame the challenge from their point of view. If, however, the problem involves other people, everyone's perspective on the challenge matters. Applying your power and authority to overcome an obstacle by brute force can create a change, but the strategy stops working when excluded stakeholders become uninspired or start to resist. It's important to consider two things about the perspectives of others when collaborating to solve a problem. First, is everyone motivated to change the situation? Second, how does your characterization of the situation relate to their needs? In the case of the messy bathroom, the shift to nagging reduction inspires everyone connected to the problem to participate.

The question generates new insights and options

Quicksand questions limit options because they originate from a desire to take action on a conclusion about the nature of the challenge. When the question focuses on motivating a change in Hannah's habits, the options are familiar and unlikely to produce a breakthrough. Surprising options that lead to breakthroughs require an insight about the situation that we haven't been paying attention to. You know you have a better question when the answers inspired by the question introduce interesting and relevant options you haven't considered.

IF YOU HAVE teenage children and you've been reading along waiting for an innovative parenting tip, you might be disappointed by our solution to the messy bathroom problem. We did nothing. The breakthrough was not related to the condition of the bathroom. The breakthrough was related to our attitude about priorities.

I'll leave Katherine out of it for the moment and admit that the messy bathroom bothered me more than it bothered her. I don't like clutter. For me, the insight gained from reframing the problem was that I love my daughter more than I dislike clutter. When I stopped obsessing about how to change Hannah's habits, I was free to think about how I wanted to spend the remaining few years of our time living in the same house. If you're parents, you know how those precious years of having young children at home end all too soon—you blink, and they're gone. They're growing up, separating, and leading their own lives, which is what they should do, but alas, it's a loss of moment-by-moment connection and love.

Coming up with ways to keep the bathroom tidy might have met some of my needs, but not the important ones. Having a conversation about working through differences in a respectful way felt more satisfying and felt like a more relevant life lesson, for all of us.

It seems almost too obvious to say, but for things to improve, something must change. What's less obvious is that one of the things available to change is ourselves. If you're stuck in freeway traffic, you could improve your situation by having something outside your control change, like a tow truck clearing away a stalled vehicle. You could improve your situation by exiting the freeway and picking an alternate route. You could also improve things by changing your attitude about your situation. Instead of thinking of yourself as stuck, you could adopt the attitude that you've been given a break in your day to catch up on a podcast or audiobook.

PART THREE

FOUR DISCIPLINES FOR NAVIGATING CHAOS

"*Labels. I stuck them on everything: 'Good.' 'Bad.' 'Right.' 'Wrong.' 'Square.' 'Hip.' 'Queer.' 'Normal.' 'Friend.' 'Enemy.' 'Success.' 'Failure.' They're easy to use. They save you the bother of thinking. Those labels stay stuck. They proliferate. They become a habit. Soon, they're covering everything, and everybody, up. You start thinking reality is the labels. Simple labels, written in permanent marker. The trouble is, reality's the opposite. Reality is nuanced, paradoxical, shifting. It's difficult. It's many things at once. That's why we're so crummy at it. People harp on about freedom. All the time. It's everywhere. There are riots and wars about what freedom is and who it's for. But the Queen of Freedom is this: to be free of labels.*"

—David Mitchell, *Utopia Avenue*

12 /

Introduction to the Four Disciplines

I've always had an uneasy relationship with expertise. I secretly aspire to know more than others about whatever subject interests me, and I am simultaneously embarrassed by the way I cling to the amount of information I amass, as if knowing things will make me popular and beloved (spoiler alert: it doesn't).

When I was in graduate school, I became interested in the process of turning students into scholars. To my dismay, I discovered that formal education produces experts, but not necessarily broad-minded thinkers. The way schooling works, the more you study, the more you're expected to specialize. By the time you're pursuing the highest degree your discipline confers, you have limited your attention to a sliver of the available scholarship.

You begin using terms of art only understood by other experts in your field. You attend conferences attended only by other scholars in your field. Your peers review what you write and decide whether others of your peers get to read it. There is a certain kind of logic at work here. After all, it is important to train people how to answer new questions and make new discoveries. We need to know whether we can count on the accuracy of their answers and effectiveness of their discoveries.

The problem with the funneling of scholarship is that you don't really become an expert in a *field* of study, you become an expert in a *well* of study. The more you learn, the deeper you dig, the higher the walls. From the bottom of a well, it's hard to notice changes in the environment. But in a chaotic, turbulent world, it's better to have strategies for getting un-stuck than to rely only on deep expertise. In 2020 we're discovering that experts at teaching students in a classroom have not been as effective as teachers who know how to adapt their practice to a world where students can't attend school because of the virus or other factors.

The four disciplines in the following chapters are a direct result of my resistance to limiting myself to one way of thinking during graduate school. I chose Saybrook University because of its reputation for combining humanist values with the study of organizational systems. I loved what I was learning and the people I was learning with. My coursework considered the way people influence their organizations and, in turn, the way organizations influence how people think and work together. When it came time to focus on a re-search topic, I decided to explore the relationship between an organization's strategy and how people in the organiza-tion prioritize their daily activities. And the more I started learning about the different ways people study organizational decision-making, the more I was being drawn into a well of scholarship.

Each well of scholarship had its own jargon and procedures. Strategic-thinking scholars invited me to consider what was going on outside the boundaries of the organization. Researchers applying systems theory offered an analytical tool kit that would help me understand what was happening inside the boundaries of the organization. The relatively new field of human-centered design science beckoned me to focus on organizational stakeholders and their needs. I was supposed to review the academic literature to demonstrate that my research would dig the well a little deeper, but I couldn't shake the feeling that choosing only one approach would not answer the question I was interested in studying.

We are poorly equipped to find a way forward amid today's turbulence because we're too comfortable in our thinking wells. Our thinking wells—our deeply held yet narrow ways of thinking about the world—have become our bunkers. We grow more isolated and divided as we continue to seek shelter from the storm.

We presume the storm is dangerous because from our limited view of the sky we only see shadowy movement across a narrow aperture. The four thinking disciplines described below prod us to the surface so that we can exchange insights with people who dwell in other wells. We might come to see that the movement reshaping the landscape is actually making the surface more hospitable for all of us.

THE FOUR THINKING DISCIPLINES

1. Explore the context

Context organizes and defines things from a perspective that is external to the situation you want to change. Exploring the context is like zooming out or sitting in the balcony to gain a view of the setting or circumstances rather than focusing on only one element. When you explore the context, you reduce the risk of missing something important.

2. Analyze structures

A structure is a well-defined combination of elements. Analyzing structures means examining the relationships among the elements that make up the structure. When you analyze structures, you avoid solving the wrong problem.

3. Empathize with needs

Psychologists have long studied human needs and motivations to understand why we make certain choices, reach certain conclusions, and demonstrate certain behaviors. Empathizing with people and their needs means allowing people's experiences and stories to inspire us. When you empathize with needs, you discover previously excluded perspectives.

4. Challenge assumptions

As we saw in Part One, our assumptions have a strong influence over how we process information and whether we succumb to blind spots and threats. Challenging assumptions means developing the awareness to notice hidden ways of thinking. When you challenge assumptions, you generate new insights and options.

BEFORE LOOKING AT some ways to build up your thinking stamina through regular application of the four disciplines, you may want to know how well you already use the disciplines when dealing with complex or uncertain situations.

Here's a quick thought experiment to try. Imagine that you have just been hired by the division of a consumer packaged-goods company that manufactures and distributes writing instruments and markers. Your first day coincides with a division-wide town hall meeting. The senior vice president of the division, a man of few words, delivers a simple message: Sell more pens.[1] Write down the first two or three questions that come to mind as you orient yourself to the task of helping sell more pens.

After codifying the four disciplines, I began categorizing the initial questions that leaders asked about the situations they wanted to change. It was surprisingly easy to connect different types of questions to each of the disciplines. When I use the sell-more-pens example in workshops or presentations, people recognize clear differences in the information they want before they formulate a plan of action.

What were the first few questions that came to mind when you imagined being asked to help sell more pens? If your initial questions had to do with the big picture, you may have wanted to learn about the division's strategy or goals. If your questions had to do with connecting the task to the company strategy or understanding trends in the industry, you were exploring the context.

Maybe you wanted to see data. You wanted to ask about sales trends, the more detailed the breakdown of sales categories, the better. An interest in understanding the health of the operating systems and routines represents a preference for analyzing structures.

Alternatively, your first consideration might have been related to the people who purchase and use the product. You may have initially formed questions about who uses the company's pens and what might be changing about their needs. If you first wanted to know more about the people who make the pens, sell the pens, or use the pens, you were drawn (so to speak) to empathizing with needs.

Finally, if your first thought had to do with changing the nature of the challenge or trying to understand the thinking behind the nature of the request, then you started by challenging assumptions. For example, your first questions might have been, Why sell more pens? Why not sell fewer pens that have a higher profit margin? Or maybe your first thought was, Why pens? Why not styluses?

All of the questions, from each of the disciplines, are potentially useful. The idea behind learning the four disciplines is that you, your team, or your organization may be most comfortable with one or two of the disciplines and consequently miss out on the benefits of the others.

Being inattentive to one or more disciplines may also represent a habit of thought that keeps you stuck, perhaps in ways you're not aware of. If you'd like to understand more about how you prefer to move from thinking to action when faced with a complex or uncertain situation, I have developed a thinking styles assessment called the Unstuck Minds Profile. You can find a description and a link to the free assessment in the Appendix.

Discipline 1: Explore the Context

People who commute to a building every day think of work as the stuff we do at an office. If work is meant to be done at an office, it makes sense that we think of being forced to do our jobs away from the office as a problem to be solved, or a temporary inconvenience. One way to meet the current moment with creativity and compassion is to explore the context you are using to understand your situation and your options.

Think about the language we use to describe the way many of us are currently doing our jobs: *work from home, remote work, telecommuting.* Matt Mullenweg, the CEO of Automattic, runs a company of over 900 people spread out across 67 countries. Automattic has never had a corporate office. It started as a distributed workforce company in 2005. Mullenweg likens the term *telecommuting* to the description of the automobile as a horseless carriage.[1]

Exploring the context means zooming out to gain a broader perspective on your situation. Organizations asking themselves how to maintain their workplace norms while following social distancing guidelines have allowed blind spots and threats to limit their thinking. Organizations applying question-ability to the changing context of the workplace are considering how sheltering-in-place has inspired ideas for liberating people from workplace norms.

TIPS FOR EXPLORING THE CONTEXT

Diversify your sources of information

Name three news media outlets you use to stay informed. If you have trouble naming at least three, you're are only getting part of the story. Of the ones you named, where are they based and who owns them? Consider getting a steady diet of news and information from one more source that provides a point of view you're not getting.

Spend time with a college student

Mental sparks fly when fresh minds confront old knowledge. Consequently, many social trends take root on college campuses. If you're looking for signals of emerging changes in preferences and priorities, college students may provide a clue. At a minimum, you become keenly aware of how your worldview differs from the emerging zeitgeist.

Follow key opinion leaders and influencers

Being a key opinion leader allows you to create self-fulfilling prophecies. If enough people seek out or pay attention to a well-known person's opinion, the opinion gains legitimacy. These days, if Bill Gates predicts a book will become a bestseller, the book becomes a bestseller because Bill Gates predicted it. (Go ahead Bill Gates, I dare you to prove me wrong.) Paying attention to what opinion leaders and influencers do or say doesn't mean that you have faith in their predictions and opinions, it just means that you are aware of what a lot of other people are paying attention to.

Learn something you don't need to know

Watch a TED talk on astronomy (assuming you aren't an astronomer) or find a podcast about attempts to bring financial services to places in the world where there are no banks. Subscribe to the question-and-answer website Quora, and follow responses to questions posted by people curious about the same topics you're interested in. Listen to any expert passionately describe the nuances of their field or practice. You never know when a random nugget of information will spur a thought about something happening in the world that can be related to a situation that matters to you.

Get curious about trends you don't understand

Fads emerge and disappear quickly in the Internet age. Thanks to the nature of the Internet, after a fad dies out, it's still a click away on any search engine. You can see Ice Bucket Challenge videos from 2014 designed to bring awareness to ALS (amyotrophic lateral sclerosis). You can find pictures of people lying face down in unusual places (known as planking) that became a craze in British media in 2009. Google the phrase *trending hashtags* anytime you want to tap into the collective conscious of social media denizens. Occasionally, you'll come across something that has captured the attention of thousands that might provide a clue about what matters to people, which might mean it should matter to you.

Read letters to shareholders in the annual reports of companies you admire

A lot of thought goes into the few pages of communication a CEO sends out annually to a company's shareholders. Warren Buffett's annual letters to Berkshire Hathaway's shareholders have been compiled in book form (they're also free online). Letters from Jeff Bezos often reference leadership lessons he has learned from experiments at Amazon. In a crisis like the current pandemic, letters to shareholders from influential companies provide a clue as to how businesses connected to you personally or to your organization's future are planning and prioritizing.

Immerse yourself in a new environment

Howard Schultz, the longtime chairman and CEO of Starbucks, was famously inspired by the espresso bar traditions of Milan. But you don't need to travel to immerse yourself in a new environment. Attend a church service in an unfamiliar neighborhood, volunteer for charity work that supports people you rarely encounter. Visit a museum or a spend time walking along a nearby nature trail. Like Schultz, you might be inspired by changing your perspective. Or you might simply benefit from freeing yourself from an environment that reinforces your limits rather than revealing possibilities.

Read counterfactual fiction

Also called alternate history fiction, counterfactual fiction speculates on the consequences of a certain historical event not happening or resulting in a different outcome. For example, Phillip Roth's 2004 novel, *The Plot Against America,* considers what might have happened if Franklin D. Roosevelt had lost the 1940 presidential election to Charles Lindbergh. Roth speculates that Lindbergh would have kept the United States out of World War II.[2] A novelist writing a counterfactual history provides a masterclass in posing the question what-if? Learning how to consider the myriad ripple effects of a single change will, at a minimum, enhance the quality of your thinking when imagining future scenarios.

Scan output from the annual meeting of the World Economic Forum

The express purpose of the Swiss-based World Economic Forum is to engage a diverse set of leaders in shaping regional and industry agendas. The forum conducts a well-known meeting each in year in Davos, Switzerland, that attracts an array of business leaders, politicians, economists, celebrities, and journalists. The forum produces articles and videos that provide an insight into the thinking of decision-makers and influencers on a range of topics related to emerging trends. The agendas and output of the Davos meetings are available free on the World Economic Forum website.

Spend time with an architect or city planner

Commercial architects and city planners have to think about the long-term implications of their decisions. Consequently, they regularly engage in speculative conversations about trends. When decisions about the design of a city or a building become a reality, choices impacting how people work and live become constrained. If you want to explore what may constrain your future options, people who are designing the places where we live might be able to provide some useful clues.

14 /

Discipline 2: Analyze Structures

A headache is an event. It creates a situation that I am motivated to change. I can take a pill, and if the headache goes away I don't need to conduct an analysis because I feel better. If, however, the headache regularly returns, I start looking for a pattern. Maybe I notice that I get the same type of headache every time I go out for a steak dinner.

Analyzing structures amounts to asking one question: Why does this pattern exist?" I might decide to discuss the headaches with a doctor, someone who specializes in the structures and systems of the human body. I might learn that the headaches are an allergic reaction to tannins, which are a component of red wine, and I have a habit of ordering a glass of red wine when I go out for a steak dinner. If I want to avoid solving the wrong problem, I need to understand how underlying structures manifest as patterns—patterns that I'm motivated to change.

Advocates for social justice and racial equity have long applied the discipline of analyzing structures to the problem of racism. The sociologist and civil rights activist W.E.B. Du Bois linked racism to capitalism at the turn of the 20th century.[1] Now that we've been reawakened to the insidious harms of racism, we can no longer afford to keep solving the wrong problem. Leaders, activists, and scholars who pay attention to patterns of injustice view policy reforms as symptoms of a seemingly immutable system. Dismantling racist structures means first shining a light on institutionalized policies and practices that benefit white Americans who have turned a blind eye to supremacist assumptions and unearned privileges.

Understanding the impacts of an underlying structure helps us avoid solving the wrong problem. However, even when we become aware of the underlying causes of harmful patterns, we may still lack the motivation to make a change. Another way to analyze structures is to consider whether a problematic pattern is the result of people being unwilling to change their convictions or let go of something they identify with.

FOR OVER 30 years the most satisfying moments in my work happened when facilitating a conversation or learning experience with a group of people in a room. I felt competent and useful as a facilitator. I learned my craft from world-class facilitators and developed philosophies about what it takes to create the conditions for insights and breakthroughs to transform individuals and groups. I identified with my work and became accustomed to doing it my way.

Even before Covid-19 isolated us, many firms who provided consulting and training services were being asked to deliver programs and facilitate meetings through web-based platforms like WebEx, Skype, and Zoom. Organizations were less willing to spend time and money pulling people offline to learn and meet. But I resisted requests to redesign meetings and learning processes so that they could be delivered virtually. I applied my rhetorical skills to argue that powerful insights emerging from a collective experience could never be replicated by interactions mediated through technology.

Was I right? Do you agree with me? Wrong questions!

Recall the chapters in Part One about blind spots and threats. One clue that I was trapped in the Inquiry Loop when it came to using technology to convene remote groups was that I wasn't just expressing an opinion, I felt emotionally invested in my opinion. Every time the topic came up, I felt defensive, cornered, and ineffectual.

The emotional response represented a pattern. To analyze the underlying mindset, I needed to consider what was causing my reaction to the topic. To consider what was causing my reaction, I needed to feel safe exploring assumptions about the relationship between my work and my self-image. Sending me to a training class on how to run an engaging Zoom meeting wasn't going to work.

Another way to avoid solving the wrong problem is to investigate whether the fear of what we might be losing helps explain a pattern of problematic behavior.

TIPS FOR ANALYZING STRUCTURES

Consider what's being lost

As discussed in Part One, our preference for preserving the status quo can be directly linked to our aversion to loss. Structures and systems are designed to maintain their own stability. When attempting to improve things, consider both the positive and the negative impacts of the future state before you begin.

The leaders of an advertising agency we work with had been touting a vision of a flexible work-from-anywhere structure months before the pandemic made the tantalizing possibilities of being liberated from the office feel more like incarceration. Some of the leaders tried to put a positive spin on working from home by suggesting that the agency had unexpectedly achieved the goal of allowing people to get work done without showing up at the office. It soon became clear that even those who preferred working from home were initially more focused on the loss of connection and involvement than the benefits of flexibility.

Share what's working

Many of us seem wired to notice gaps, inefficiencies, and flaws. Engineers are trained to make things better, so they focus on opportunities for improvement. We can learn and develop solutions by discovering the root causes of success, not just from uncovering the root causes of a problem. Taking note of what's working not only inspires solutions, it restores confidence.

Draw diagrams

Diagramming elements can be a powerful tool for analyzing structures. There are a variety of specific methodologies for diagramming structural elements (causal loop diagrams, fishbone diagrams, flowcharts, mind maps, etc.). They all share a common purpose. An analytical diagram helps us visualize how elements are organized and connected. You can look for mind-mapping or data-visualization software online, but a blank sheet of paper or a whiteboard works too.

Try brainstorming elements of a problem or opportunity onto sticky notes and then arranging them so that you can draw lines between elements that are connected. An element that seems to be at the hub of a lot of other elements is a good candidate for where to focus your analysis. A useful diagram makes it easier to see causes, or influential elements. When you think through a complex situation with the help of a diagram, you will feel less overwhelmed. Without a way to visualize elements and their relationships, we end up thinking about all aspects of a situation at once, treating all aspects of a situation as equally important—or else we risk missing important elements altogether.

Learn about national cultures

The idea of nations as political units into which the world is divided has only been the norm since the mid-20th century. It makes more sense to think of common social cultures as belonging to societies that developed organically rather than belonging to nations whose boundaries are drawn and rearranged based on politics, wars, and geography. Nevertheless, we have become accustomed to identifying ourselves with our nations, and much of the research on global cultures connects our inclinations to our national heritage.

One of the most well-regarded and frequently cited frameworks for understanding global culture and values is Hofstede's cultural dimensions theory.[2] The Hofstede model considers national norms related to:

- The role of clearly established hierarchy in how people view power
- The value of individualism versus collectivism
- The society's tolerance for ambiguity versus certainty
- The importance a society places on behavior consistent with traditional gender roles
- The fostering of virtues related to the past and present versus an orientation toward future rewards
- Whether the society indulges citizens in the gratification of their desires or restrains citizens by means of strict standards of behavior

National cultures represent foundational mindsets that help explain patterns of behavior. Despite the best efforts of xenophobic politicians, we cannot restrict our interest in people to only those within our borders if we hope to avoid getting stuck in our thinking.

See patterns

Recognizing patterns is a key step in analyzing the structures that might be responsible for keeping you stuck. When becoming aware of a situation someone is motivated to change (a problem), consider whether the situation is an isolated incident or if it is part of a larger pattern. To see patterns requires the ability to generalize or abstract out attributes and characteristics rather than focusing exclusively on the specifics of a given situation.

If you're watching a TV show and you notice that the plot seems similar to the plot of another story, you are seeing a pattern. As you take in information or make your way in the world, practice scanning and patterning. What are you seeing more of? What are you seeing less of? As you walk the aisles of your grocery store, which products are being given more shelf space and which products are being given less shelf space? What are the most popular topics being taken up by current writers of business books?

Work awake

Most of the activities we undertake in the course of a day get accomplished without giving them much thought. We don't have to focus when engaged in the habitual activities we've mastered. We operate on autopilot when driving our cars unless something changes in the environment. If driving conditions become dangerous, we stop multitasking and concentrate; we become more aware of our surroundings and the moves we're making.

Working awake means choosing to place more of your attention on routine work tasks. Sometimes we get stuck because the environment has changed, but we continue operating on autopilot.

As an example, consider your routines when it comes to the various forms of written communication you use throughout the day (email, text, group communication platforms, social media posts, etc.). If you tend to power through messages quickly, you have likely developed a style of responding. It's also likely that when you start communicating with someone who doesn't know you well, you give more thought to how you express your message. If you don't work awake when sending messages, it's likely that you've had the experience of being misinterpreted. A team can work awake by periodically assessing whether their routines produce the desired outcomes. When you make a habit of thinking about your habits, you're more likely to notice when underlying structures and mindsets need to shift.

Study big decisions

Try to remember the last momentous decision you made (to make a substantial purchase, to change jobs, to move, etc.). How did it feel as you considered your options before reaching a conclusion about what to do? How did you know that you were done thinking about options, that you had made up your mind? It's difficult to put yourself back in your prior frame of mind once the decision has been made and you are living with the consequences. Gaining insight into someone's experience of deliberating—especially someone who has to make consequential decisions—clarifies the influences of mindsets and structures.

Journal your own deliberations next time you need to make a consequential decision that will impact others. What are the most influential factors? Are you more concerned about reaching a high-quality conclusion or about gaining acceptance and support for the decision? What previous experiences have shaped your thinking about the decisions?

During the Cuban missile crisis of 1962, the U.S. military advocated for a bombing attack of the missile sites being installed by the Soviet Union. According to presidential historian Robert Dallek, the Joint Chiefs of Staff at the time, who had served under General Eisenhower during World War II, shared a mindset about the value of decisive and overwhelming use of force, up to and including the deployment of the nuclear arsenal. As commanders during the war they had experienced the successes of invasions and bombing campaigns. In contrast, President Kennedy had served as the commander of a patrol torpedo boat that capsized after a collision with a Japanese destroyer. Kennedy and his crew spent 15 hours in the water, made it to a small island, and were rescued six days later. Significant and instructive deliberations went into the ultimate decision not to bomb the missile sites in Cuba.[3] Studying the deliberations helps us recognize the power of underlying influences implicit in decision-making discussions.

Learn about data science

Data science involves a variety of methods and disciplines to derive knowledge and insights from both structured and unstructured data. More and more of our everyday actions involve interfacing with connected machines. Additionally, more and more of the objects we use have embedded chips and sensors that track our behaviors. I can wear a device that will track my posture, and I can sip from a water bottle that will track my hydration habits. Our locations are tracked whenever we bring our mobile devices with us. Whatever we type into a search bar, whatever gets scanned when we make a purchase, the shows and videos we watch—all are part of a traceable life story, a permanent digital wake made up of bits and bytes.

Just as we avoid solving the wrong problem by noticing patterns and then interpreting the patterns by analyzing underlying structures, data scientists write computer programs to detect patterns in the vast ocean of data created by the collective behaviors of connected humans. Whether for good or evil, the patterns detected by data scientists get applied by organizations, agencies, and governments to influence us. Being conversant in how big data is used and what data scientists are learning will augment your own pattern recognition skills.

Anticipate potential consequences

One of the benefits of analyzing structures is that it puts you in a better position to predict the consequences of taking actions. When the best chess players consider their next move, they think through the various consequences of their opponent's responses. Because the underlying structure of chess limits options, the best human chess players can think 10 to 15 moves ahead. The underlying structures of our organizations constrain options somewhat, but not enough to confidently forecast all the outcomes of a decision or action. It's as if a player's chess pieces had free will and human emotions.

The unpredictability of an organization's reactions to change does not mean that the exercise of considering various what-if scenarios is pointless. Anticipating consequences requires you to expose some of your assumptions and working theories about the organization. When others join in the exercise, you learn how people think and what they prioritize. Playing with future scenarios helps you and your organization become more adaptable as the future unfolds. You may also recognize leading indicators of a change before others because you've imagined a variety of possibilities.

Personify the system

As Lou Gerstner discovered when he took the reins at IBM, organizational cultures are powerful stabilizing forces that can take on a life of their own. In fact, we personify cultures without giving it much thought. We apply adjectives to sports teams; the Oakland Raiders have been described as "tough" and "mean." We think of cities as having personalities: New York is vibrant; Paris is romantic.

We have also defined a problem as a situation someone wants to change. Combining these ideas can lead to interesting insights about the nature of what may be keeping a system stuck. Imagine personifying a system or culture you are part of and that you experience as dissatisfying in some way. You may be motivated to change your situation, but the system may seem unchangeable. If you were to personify the system, you could then ask whether the system is experiencing a situation it is motivated to change.

I spent several years conducting leadership development workshops in a technology company with a very strong culture. The culture was a reflection of the founder, who to this day remains the chairman and CEO. The company recognized the need to shift its focus from hardware and devices to software and solutions. The transformation would require a shift of focus from technical excellence to customer service. If I were to personify the system, I might use words like *entrepreneurial, technically brilliant problem-solvers, action-oriented, brash*. The leaders I worked with understood that selling solutions required greater sensitivity to customer needs. Personifying the culture as a technically brilliant, insensitive, action-oriented problem-solver (think Tony Stark, the Marvel superhero known as Iron Man) clarified the challenge. Asking what it would take for brash technologists to be motivated to change how they work feels less daunting than asking how do we change our culture?

Discipline 3: Empathize with Needs

Several years ago, a colleague and I worked with a large public school district in Florida. The district had recently awarded a janitorial services contract to an outsourcing company. The company brought us in to facilitate a series of meetings to align groups on the steps required to transition janitorial services from site-based control to the outsourcing company.

One of the major disagreements that needed to be settled had to do with management of the janitors in the school buildings. Previously, the school principals were involved in all aspects of hiring and managing the performance of the janitors working in their buildings. The outsourcing company wanted to take over management of the janitors, teach them new techniques and routines, and deploy them across the district. The challenge was framed by the question of who would be managing the janitors.

The outsourcing company pointed out that the contract with the school district clearly stated they would manage the janitorial workforce. The school principals objected that they needed site-based control over anyone working in their buildings.

What we should now recognize right away is that the question—Who manages the janitors?—is too narrow and framed as an either/or choice.

We asked the school principals about their needs, worries, beliefs, and assumptions. We discovered that the principals feared that newly hired janitors might not be required to go through the district's hiring process, which included security checks and drug screening. They worried that something would happen during the school day requiring the immediate attention of a janitor and one might not be onsite. The principals wanted any janitor working in their school building to feel like a valued and trusted member of the school staff.

In the end, instead of debating who should manage the janitors, we were able to redefine the challenge as how we might ensure the principals felt comfortable with the janitors working in their buildings and that a trusted janitor would be available to respond to immediate needs during school hours.

Asking the second question allowed us to generate several options, which became part of the outsourcing contract. Recall from our discussion of threat responses in Chapter 4 that in the face of change, we naturally focus on what is being lost. The principals were being told that they were losing control, flexibility, predictability, and authority. It's not surprising that they insisted on maintaining the status quo. By stepping away from the original framing of the challenge, we made it safe for the principals to express their concerns and needs.

Principals care about academic performance; they don't wake up every morning thinking, *I can't wait to manage the custodial staff*. Sometimes the simple act of setting aside the existing challenge definition provides an opening for people to remind themselves of what really matters.

Empathizing with needs is ultimately about human dignity. We don't get unstuck by imposing our preferred solutions on others. We get unstuck by turning an insight about what people need into a solution that will motivate people to adopt a change. Exploring the context helps us identify external elements we should not ignore. Analyzing structures helps us learn about the inner workings of the situation we want to change. Empathizing with needs helps us learn about who is motivated to get unstuck and what motivates them. Focusing on what people actually need versus focusing on what we want them to have is not only more influential, it's more ethical. Theodore Levitt, a well-known professor at Harvard Business School, in writing about the importance of focusing on needs, quoted promotions manager Leo McGivena: "Last year one million quarter-inch drill bits were sold—not because people wanted quarter-inch drill bits, but because they wanted quarter-inch holes."[1]

TIPS FOR EMPATHIZING WITH NEEDS

Discover shared interests

In their 1981 bestselling book on negotiation, *Getting to Yes: Negotiating Agreement Without Giving In*, Roger Fisher and

William Ury made an important distinction between "positions" and "interests."[2]

In a discussion, conflict, or negotiation, your position represents the solution or outcome you *say* you want. Your interests are the *true* needs and desires that cause you to advocate for your position. For example, say I hold the position that the family should vacation in northern Arizona next summer. My interests might include a desire to get away from the heat of Texas, a desire to share the experience of walking through an inspiring landscape with my wife and daughters, and a desire to avoid crowds. When we focus on our positions, we can unintentionally limit our options. When we explore underlying interests, we invite a variety of options. There are plenty of ways to get out of Texas, avoid crowds, and hike with my family other than by visiting northern Arizona.

When we empathize with needs, we look for excluded perspectives to help us get unstuck. We may think we've included a stakeholder's perspective by hearing their position. In fact, we may have missed an opportunity to learn from diverse perspectives because we're left to make assumptions about interests when all we have are a collection of positions. When an activist says that we should defund the police, it's tempting to pass judgment on the idea rather than explore the interests being served by the idea. Perhaps the activist's comment was motivated by feelings of hopelessness and a belief that policy reforms and training don't produce sustainable improvements or lead to equitable systems of justice. Imagine the differences between a conversation about whether or not to defund the police and a conversation about how to ensure that citizens feel safe, protected, and confident that helpful, professional responders will intervene appropriately.

Learn from outliers

You might be surprised to learn that marketing firms and design firms hire people who have degrees in anthropology. Anthropologists study human behavior in the context of our societies, past and present. Design and marketing firms understand that the most successful products, services, and messages are the ones that connect with the desires, needs, and motivations of people. One way to develop new insights and options when stuck is to study people as if you were an anthropologist. When people engage in interesting and unusual behaviors, they give us a glimpse into interesting and unusual needs or desires. If we allow ourselves to be inspired by what we witness, we might just see a new way forward.

Tim Brown, the former CEO of the global design firm IDEO and author of the book *Change by Design*, wrote about IDEO's focus on "extreme users":

> By concentrating solely on the bulge at the center of the bell curve ... we are more likely to confirm what we already know than learn something new and surprising. For insights at that level we need to head for the edges, the places where we expect to find "extreme" users who live differently, think differently, and consume differently.[3]

Brown tells the story of IDEO's design work for the Swiss company Zyliss. Zyliss engaged IDEO to design a new line of kitchen tools. The IDEO team started by observing children and professional chefs—not because children and professional chefs represented the target market for the Zyliss utensils but because chefs and kids have interesting needs and constraints when they use kitchen tools. For example, IDEO learned how someone who lacks the typical strength of an able-bodied adult struggles to use certain utensils like a can opener or a pizza slicer. IDEO observed the demands for keeping utensils clean and sanitary when in constant use in a commercial kitchen. When you see the finished Zyliss kitchen gadgets, you can easily trace back certain design choices that were inspired by discovering excluded perspectives.

Analyze TV commercials

Do you know who spends a lot of time thinking about the motivations and unarticulated needs of people? Advertisers. Why are ads for insurance companies built around real or fictional characters? Why do commercials for automobiles rarely focus on the features of the engine? Why is that you're never sure what a perfume ad is about until a sexy voice with a French accent mentions the name of the product in the last few seconds of the commercial? Advertising is expensive and companies work hard to avoid wasting their money.

Advertisers tap into people's desires, frustrations, and fears to influence their purchasing behavior. Empathizing with needs is about seeking to understand people's desires, frustrations, and fears in order to get unstuck. The goal is to use your empathic savvy to get inspired and learn, not to manipulate or promote your own point of view.

Assume reasonableness

When teaching facilitation skills, I'll often ask workshop participants to list behaviors they find challenging or disruptive during meetings. Not surprisingly, people have no difficulty generating a long list. I then ask, "These people who show up late, get distracted, have sidebar conversations, are argumentative or opinionated—who are these people?" I pause dramatically and wait for some enlightened participant to admit that we all demonstrate these behaviors. I point out that when I show up late, or get distracted, or engage in sidebar conversations, or become argumentative, I have a good reason. Maybe I'm overbooked, or stressed out, or bored, or passionate. If I understand why I might exhibit disruptive behaviors, it helps me see disruptive behaviors in others as reasonable. I don't have to like what I see, and I don't have to agree with what I hear. I also don't have to treat the behavior as a personal attack. Maybe I can learn something important by responding with compassion and curiosity.

If I notice someone checking their phone while I'm making a presentation, I might feel disrespected and maybe a little angry. If I remind myself to assume reasonableness, I shift from being captured by the emotions to being thoughtful about the emotions. When I become thoughtful, I can recall that I too have exhibited the same behavior when I'm anxious about something happening outside the meeting. If I pause for empathy and curiosity before engaging with the person checking their phone, my response will be compassionate and measured.

Take in a stranger's story

Great biographies and memoirs help us understand the inner lives of people. Unless you are lucky enough to have close relationships with a diverse group of friends or colleagues, it can be hard to develop empathy for worldviews and backgrounds different from your own. Stories introduce us to real people and historical figures in a multidimensional and nuanced way. Reading, for example, about Tara Westover's upbringing in a survivalist Mormon family in her memoir, *Educated,* introduced me to characters and ways of thinking I would have never encountered.[4]

Watch the novelist Chimamanda Ngozi Adichie's TED talk called "The Danger of a Single Story."[5] Adichie describes her experience growing up in Nigeria and her encounters with people when she attended university in the United States. She describes the tendencies we all have to fit people different from us into the single story we impose on people when we see them as representatives of a group rather than individuals with their own stories.

Visit someplace that feels uninviting

Have you ever found yourself in a place or circumstance that left you feeling like you didn't belong? Imagine if that was your daily experience. Maybe you need a wheelchair to get around and you regularly encounter obstacles because public spaces were not designed with you in mind. Maybe you're a racial minority in a society dominated by people who don't look like you, who disregard or maybe even fear you.

Developing your ability to empathize with others' needs will be enhanced by firsthand experience of being ignored or discounted. You don't need lengthy or risky exposure to uncomfortable surroundings to acquire a touchstone experience. The simple act of reflecting on what it would be like to make your way in unfamiliar territory will connect you to the value of empathizing with needs. How would you go about making a productive contribution if the people you work with didn't acknowledge or include you?

Develop habits of inclusion

Building capability to empathize with needs might require a hard look at your current habits and behaviors. Will Schutz, an American psychologist, author, and creator of the Fundamental Interpersonal Relations Orientation theory and the FIRO-B assessment, describes *significance* as the primary feeling associated with our need for inclusion. For Schutz, to feel significant is to "know that I make a difference, am an important person, am meaningful and worthwhile."[6]

Pay close attention over the course of a week to the ways in which you help people feel significant and the ways in which you diminish people's feelings of significance. Perhaps you've never made eye contact with the members of the crew who clean the building you work in. Maybe you're focused on your phone even when a clerk or cashier is ringing up your purchases. You can't empathize with the needs of people who are invisible to you. People who feel invisible to others might eventually stop believing they have a right to significance.

Pay attention to hubs and peripheries

The people who have access to the greatest variety of perspectives can be found at the hubs and peripheries of your organization. Someone at a hub becomes a central communication point, either because of their role or because of their personality. An executive assistant is often a hub of information and activity because they also act as a gatekeeper for a decision-maker. Someone at the periphery of an organization has a role that puts them in regular contact with external professionals. Salespeople and people in an organization's purchasing function often hear about what's happening in other organizations before anyone else does.

When I worked for Interaction Associates, I would often chat with Marie. Among her many duties, Marie was responsible for processing expense reports. Marie was also a beloved figure who cared deeply about the firm and everyone who worked there. On an organizational chart, Marie's role would not seem to have a great deal of formal authority—nor was Marie invited to senior team meetings. Nevertheless, Marie was at the hub of a lot of communication and information.

A few years ago, Marie noticed an unusual volume of expense report forms over a period of several months from a talented colleague of mine named Michael. Michael's expenses included global travel and lodging in a variety of countries in different regions of the world. Marie made an offhand comment to another of my colleagues; she was worried that Michael might be getting burned out by what appeared to Marie like a set of challenging global assignments undertaken at a grueling pace. A few weeks later, Michael left the firm.

In organizations, we often link the value of someone's perspective to the strategic importance of their role. But it isn't necessarily just the usual suspects who have strategic importance. Who in your organization knows more about what's going on inside and outside your function than you? How might hearing more from them help you get unstuck or prevent you from getting stuck?

Create psychological safety

The construct known as *psychological safety* moved from the relative obscurity of academic literature into the spotlight after Charles Duhigg wrote an article for the *New York Times Magazine* in 2016 about a Google's team's quest to understand team effectiveness.[7] The article highlighted the research of Harvard Business School professor Amy Edmondson, who defines psychological safety as a "shared belief held by members of a team that the team is safe for interpersonal risk-taking."[8]

One of the biggest insights coming from the Google team's research, code-named Project Aristotle, is that people want their team members to understand who they really are and not just interact with the version of themselves they express in the workplace. When it feels safe to take interpersonal risks, people get a more complete picture of each other; this in turn builds trust and rapport. To empathize with needs requires an ability to understand the unarticulated or hidden needs that may only surface during an interaction that feels psychologically safe.

Role-model vulnerability

Professor, author, and lecturer Brené Brown has made empathy and vulnerability cool. As of this writing, her TED talk "The Power of Vulnerability" has been viewed over 48 million times.[9] Brown's research centers on our relationship with uncertainty and emotional risk. Her message is connected to the research on psychological safety. Namely, the path to fulfillment and breakthroughs passes through a space where you risk exposure to the judgments of others.

Building your capacity to empathize with needs includes getting comfortable demonstrating vulnerability. Most people will only explore out loud their real needs in the presence of someone who demonstrates empathy. One of the most effective ways to lessen people's reluctance to express their needs is to go first. Showing vulnerability to others nurtures openness in others.

Discipline 4: Challenge Assumptions

Global crises have devastating impacts on people's lives—some more than others. They also have a devastating impact on our comfortable worldviews—for some people more than others. Baby Boom and Gen-X adults have happily coexisted with a set of assumptions that are now up for debate as part of our public social discourse. It may feel like chaos, but it will more than likely be remembered as progress.

You can't challenge assumptions if you don't see the assumptions in the first place. Like a fish swimming in water, we don't notice what we are born into because we can't observe ourselves from a different vantage point. We can, however, learn from a review of what we once assumed to be true but have revised with experience or modified based on a transformative insight.

Allow me to share a few assumptions I have held and abandoned:

- There are only two genders.
- Law enforcement and punishment are the best ways to ensure public safety.
- Each successive generation will enjoy a more socially just society than the previous one.
- Only intelligent, well-informed, emotionally mature adults can be elected president of the United States.

When I look at the list, I notice two things: First, when I held these assumptions, I thought about them as the truth about the world. Second, when I look at them now, I recognize that they came to me because of my upbringing, my culture, my race, and other features of my identity. If I had been born someone else or somewhere else, I might never have accepted the assumptions as truths about the world.

I never consciously adopted the assumptions; they simply showed up as part of my default programming—which leads me to wonder what else constrains how I think. The discipline of challenging assumptions invites you, your team, and your organization to consider what may be constraining thoughts about your current situation and possibilities for your future. The tips below will help you notice and challenge the assumptions tangled up with how you, your team, or your organization operates.

TIPS FOR CHALLENGING ASSUMPTIONS

Seek out a reverse mentor

One of the best ways to reveal and change our innate assumptions is to set up a reverse mentoring relationship. The traditional mentorship model in organizations provides younger, less experienced employees with access to career advice from more experienced senior leaders. A newer twist on traditional mentorship matches senior leaders with people who have more recently joined the organization.[1]

Reverse mentorship programs provide the more experienced leaders with input from a generation that is technologically savvy and attuned to social trends—and that is and will be the driving force behind social change. One of the defining characteristics of any generation is the distinctiveness of its values and worldviews. No one may be better equipped to challenge the assumptions driving your approach to getting unstuck than people who are entering a system that they did not create and do not endorse. Younger generations will more quickly notice how a culture they have joined constrains or rewards certain behaviors and ways of thinking.

Check the label

Labeling things allows us to avoid thinking too hard about exceptions and subtle differences. It also speeds up communication with people who use the same labels. I can communicate meaningfully with most people by referring to points of light in the night sky as stars even when some of the objects I'm talking about are planets.

Labels can also inhibit our thinking. First, labels activate confirmation bias. When we label a person as smart or responsible, we notice characteristics that validate the label and filter out characteristics that contradict it. Second, we make judgments and predictions about individuals or situations that fit our label: She'll be here on time. She's very responsible.

Labels become dangerous when we mix up conclusions about the individual with conclusions about the label. During the 2020 presidential race, politicians on the right wanted voters to conflate Joe Biden and Kamala Harris with labels like "radical left" and "socialist." Politicians on the left wanted voters to conflate Donald Trump with labels like "fascist" and "racist." If you notice an emotional response to reading one of the last two sentences, you are experiencing firsthand the power of labels.

Labels are attractive to our thinking in the same way that sugary desserts are attractive to our palate, and they are equally unhealthy. If you find yourself at an impasse in your thinking about something or someone, consider the labels you use. What assumptions about the label may not fully describe the particular case under consideration? When you notice a characteristic that doesn't fit the label, you have a couple of options. You can dismiss the characteristic as an exception that proves the rule, or you can acknowledge that all labels have fuzzy boundaries when you scrutinize them.

Listen for worldviews

When helping people get unstuck by challenging their assumptions, you'll need to learn how to listen for someone's worldview or underlying beliefs. When people feel stuck, simply asking them to name their assumptions rarely works. Being stuck often amounts to being misled by our own thinking.

First, learn to distinguish an observation from an interpretation. An observation describes what I detect with my senses. An interpretation results from assigning meaning to what I observe. If I notice that someone on the team has not contributed any opinions or ideas during the last several meetings (observation), I might infer that the person is shy—that's an interpretation. As noted above, the interpretation often comes in the form of a label.

Next, learn to distinguish between an interpretation and an underlying belief. Interpretations are specific to a situation: He is shy. This meeting is boring. That plan won't work. Underlying beliefs are generic and comprehensive: People who don't speak up are shy. Engaging meetings involve a lot of debate. Plans without measurable objectives are doomed to failure.

Mind the measures

As a parent, do you want your kid to be an A student or do you want your kid to be well educated? The careful reader will recognize the question as a quicksand question of the either/or variety. Those who saw the trap in the question get an A. Of course, I'm not really asking a question; I'm making a point. Metrics are ubiquitous. We have become so accustomed to metrics that we often confuse the metric with the thing we are measuring. Organizations and public institutions devise metrics to better understand the health of the system and to better understand distinctions in performance.

Sometimes metrics start off as a way to improve things but then over time become a means for controlling things. We want to track academic test scores to improve comprehension and teaching methods. Over time, the test scores get linked to school ratings, faculty compensation, and property taxes.

The distinction I am making between measuring for improvement and measuring for control is elegantly explained by a principle known as Goodhart's Law. A popularized statement of the law goes like this: When a measure becomes a target, it ceases to be a good measure. Charles Goodhart's original formulation from a 1984 book on monetary policy in the United Kingdom is less pithy, but more consistent with the distinction I am trying to make.

"Any observed statistical regularity," Goodhart wrote, "will tend to collapse once pressure is placed upon it for control purposes."[2] Applying the law to the context of test scores in public schools, one might argue that putting pressure on teachers and students to meet test score performance targets will reduce the degree to which the test scores can be used to reach valid conclusions about what students are learning. Metrics hide assumptions about what matters.

One path to getting unstuck is to expose the assumptions behind the metrics in order to discuss whether what's being measured still matters and whether the metric we've chosen still leads to valid conclusions.

Reflect on your triggers

Feeling our emotions makes us human, and psychologists generally consider it healthier to experience our emotions rather than suppress them. Emotional reactions can also be instructive and developmental. If we witness something that violates societal norms, we would expect to have a strong emotional reaction. When we notice that a situation or behavior triggers us, while others seem less affected, we have been presented with an opportunity to learn something about ourselves.

In my case, when I hear someone express judgments as unassailable truths, my limbic system kicks in and I have to exert control over my emotions if I want to productively interact with that person. It would be easier to write the person off as a blowhard or dogmatic. Labeling the person is a more tempting option than working to understand the person. A more useful exercise that bolsters thinking stamina is to focus less on what I dislike about the person's behavior and focus more on what I can learn about myself by reflecting on my reaction.

When you reflect on behaviors and situations that trigger your emotions, you build up your self-awareness. Even if you don't fully understand what is getting under your skin, you will have built up some resistance to future emotional harm. Simply reflecting on your reactions will prepare you to collaborate with people, including those whose behavior you find challenging.

Why do expressions of emphatic certainty bother me? This book is littered with clues. I'm making a case for adopting a beginner's mind. I've posited that in times of change and uncertainty, not knowing what to do can be a superpower. I've tarnished expertise and ennobled philosophical doubt. I yearn to be right, but I've decided it's better to be questioning. I've gone so far as to hijack the negative term *questionability* and turn it into the positive trait of question-ability. Naturally, I'm triggered by displays of what I consider dogmatism. Psychologists would likely describe my reaction as projection—but enough about me. The tip being offered here is to do the hard work of learning what makes you tick. If you can see it in yourself, you can transform what annoys you into compassion for yourself and compassion for others.

Start from scratch

One way to disempower hidden assumptions is to engage in a thought experiment that starts with throwing away everything about your current situation and starting over from one foundational principle. Let's say you're trying to figure out how you want to spend your time when you retire. You start to think about it and immediately become overwhelmed. There are too many options, overly complex financial considerations, various family and friends living in different places. Each of the particulars is rife with assumptions that may limit or misdirect how you think about things.

Now imagine that none of your current circumstances exist. You can create any situation, but you have to start with a foundational principle. What do you want to organize your desired future around? Maybe you'd answer that more than anything you want to be a consistent presence in your grandchildren's lives. Once you clarify the starting assumption, it provides criteria for other choices. Being a consistent presence in the lives of your grandchildren probably means prioritizing health and proximity to family over living in a beachfront condo in a different country.

Learn about your implicit associations

You can't challenge an assumption you're unaware of. The topic of implicit bias or unconscious bias has gained a lot of traction in connection with social justice and racial equity. Many of the assumptions that guide our conclusions and behaviors sneak into our operating systems uninvited. Like the air we breathe, ideas and associations imperceptibly permeate our waking lives. If we are bombarded by images of Black men and crime scenes, we eventually form an association that unfairly becomes part of the way we make sense of the world.

Mahzarin Banaji, Anthony Greenwald, and Brian Nosek are researchers and professors who developed the Implicit Association Test.[3] You can take the IAT by visiting https://implicit.harvard.edu/implicit/takeatest.html. The IAT helps you learn about the assumptions and associations that guide your opinions and behaviors—assumptions and associations that you may be either unwilling or unable to talk about. The IAT powerfully demonstrates inconsistencies in what we profess about our associations and the actual associations our brains are making unconsciously. For example, you may think you do not make any judgments about people based solely on whether they are able-bodied or have a noticeable disability.

You can take the Disability IAT to learn whether you make implicit associations based on disability.

Listen as an ally to an adversary

Interaction Associates teaches people to think about the difference between listening to someone as an ally and listening to someone as an adversary. When I listen as an adversary, I listen critically. I consider whether I agree or disagree with what is being said, and I'm on the lookout for gaps in logic, inconsistencies, or baseless assumptions. When I listen as an ally, I'm serving the speaker. My purpose is to help the speaker feel understood. When I listen as an ally, I want to help the speaker make sense and deepen how we both understand what is being talked about.

If you want to build your thinking stamina and get better at challenging assumptions (yours and others), listen to someone whose politics you despise. Before you try this with a neighbor who has a different yard sign than you, watch a recorded speech. When you hear a statement that you disagree with or that triggers an emotional response, hit the pause button and think about how you'd answer the following questions:

- What impact does the speaker want to have by making the statement?
- What does the speaker believe about the intended audience?
- What matters to the speaker? Why does that matter to him or her?

- What would be another way of making the statement that would feel more reasonable to you?
- What upbringing or circumstances would lead someone to resonate with the speaker's statement?

Now, would you be willing to share your answers with the speaker? If you couldn't shift your mindset from adversary to ally, your answers are likely tainted. If you were able to imagine exploring with the speaker a deeper understanding of their perspective, your answers would lead to a productive exchange. You might even be able to get a fair hearing of your own perspective. If we are only capable of understanding people we agree with, our society is doomed.

Check your sources

We need actual intelligence, not artificial intelligence, to protect us from false or manipulative information. The Internet makes sharing information a little too easy. New advances in machine learning and digital manipulation have made artificial events indistinguishable from documented events. A *deep fake,* for example, is video that appears to be a recording of, say, a speech by a politician, but is in fact a convincing creation—a vastly more complex version of the famously altered *National Geographic* cover that repositioned the Pyramids of Giza.

A startling example of a deep fake has been created by a team of MIT media artists and artificial intelligence companies.[4] You can view the deep fake at moondisaster.org. In 1969, as Apollo 11 was approaching the lunar surface for the historic landing, William Safire, then one of President

Nixon's speechwriters, wrote a speech for Nixon to deliver in the event a disaster befell the mission. The deep fake uses the text of the speech that was never delivered to create a disturbingly realistic fake event. At the website, you'll see Richard Nixon deliver the speech as if it's archival footage.

If you come across media or messages that you can't wait to share with your friends and followers, first check your impulse, then check the sources. The impulse may be a clue. If you're eager to share it because it riles you up or makes you giddy, consider what you know about the source. Who put the information out and why?

Externalize your thinking

If I'm working with a group to align on a proposal, I might say, "We appear to be agreed." If I wanted to externalize my thinking, I could say a bit more: "I usually assume that when no one raises an objection, we're agreed." In the second case, you're helping the group understand how you reached your conclusion. You are also giving people who process information differently than you an opening to express their perspectives.

If you are among the former office workers who find themselves meeting online, you have probably learned the hard way to be more explicit and disciplined about externalizing your thinking. Saying, "We appear to be agreed" when everyone is in the same room is less risky than the same statement made during a conference call or a Zoom meeting. It's always been a good idea to share your thinking when collaborating with a group. When collaborating with a distributed workforce, it's imperative.

17 /

Restoring Creativity
and Compassion

We don't need to feel helpless when we don't know what to do. To be helpless is to be at the mercy of something outside your control. If you allow uncertainty and lack of confidence to paralyze you, you won't be able to fulfill the mission I've set forth in this book.

We can choose how we respond. This was Viktor Frankl's message to us from the concentration camps. Frankel, a neurologist, psychiatrist, and Holocaust survivor wrote:

We who lived in concentration camps can remember men who walked through the huts, comforting others, giving away their last piece of bread. They may have been few in number, but they offer sufficient proof that everything can be taken from a man but one thing: the last of the human freedoms—to choose one's attitude in any given set of circumstances, to choose one's own way.[1]

The freedom to choose how we respond is available, but it is not easy to access under challenging circumstances. As Frankl pointed out, the prisoners who chose to comfort others were "few in number."

To choose how we respond means liberating ourselves from the confining influences of the Inquiry Loop. We diminish our ability to respond when we protect our beliefs and assumptions from being challenged by unfamiliar interactions and diverse perspectives. We diminish our ability to respond when we choose appetizing simplicity over harder-to-digest nuance, ambiguity, and complexity.

We protect our capacity to respond to uncertainty by adopting thinking disciplines that preserve our beginner's mind. Consider for a moment how it feels when you don't know what to do. The beginner isn't bothered by not knowing what to do. Chaos doesn't incapacitate the beginner. The beginner is eager to learn and explore. The expert who doesn't know what to do is at a loss. The beginner has nothing to lose.

In the same way that a vaccine immunizes us against disease, I want to build up our immunity to closed-mindedness. The current epidemic of closed-mindedness leaves us vulnerable to lies and simplistic platitudes. The most dangerous virus is the one that makes us susceptible to dogmatism and attention-grabbing. Easy answers in difficult times are no answers at all. When our stamina for discernment has been lowered, we accommodate the most easily digestible, the briefest, the loudest, the most outrageous. We become susceptible to messages that light up our limbic system by appealing directly to our emotions. It's no coincidence that we refer to attention-grabbing media as viral.

I find it difficult to feel compassion for people whose behavior violates the principles I live by, and I suspect many reading this book have the same problem. Yet one of my principles is rooted in valuing growth and development. Growth and development in turbulent times means helping people feel safe, including people we oppose. It's difficult, but worth the effort.

The turbulent times we're living in now scare us because the future is uncertain, and each new day brings upsetting news. We know that being hypervigilant while maintaining a heightened state of anxiety takes its toll on the body. It also takes its toll on our ability to meet the moment with open minds. If venturing into unfamiliar territory means leaving a part of us behind, we need to feel safe enough to reassess beliefs with which we identify.

Trump supporters warn us that Joe Biden's America won't be safe. Many of the white majority don't feel safe when the conversation turns to defunding the police. Some people don't feel safe gathering together during a pandemic, while others don't feel safe trusting the advice of government institutions or the media. Our political leaders are starting to pay attention to the consequences of disaffected voters who feel unsafe because they feel misunderstood and devalued. During the 2020 U.S. presidential campaign, we heard the word *empathy* as much as we heard the word *economy*.

If learning to deal with uncertainty and complexity feels threatening, very few of us will make the effort. The result will be a slow depletion of the last of our human freedoms: the freedom to choose how we respond. The practices and exercises in this book can help us adapt to chaos and instability and inspire us to meet the uncertainty of the moment with compassion and creativity.

ACKNOWLEDGMENTS

A community of talented, passionate, and interesting people inspired, redirected, and nurtured the manuscript that became this book. Artisans and advisors teamed up to make the finished product readable, accurate, and well designed. Friends, family, and colleagues invested time and energy discussing ideas with me, commenting on early drafts, and cheering me on.

The editing process has taken place during a year of disasters, disruptions, confrontations, and setbacks. Even the most hopeful and optimistic among us have experienced moments of despair. Still, as I reflect on the help I've received in the development of this book, I not only feel grateful, I feel reassured. I'm heartened by the creativity and compassion people have contributed.

Alan Rinzler, my acerbic and principled editor, turned me and my manuscript inside out. His initial response to the first draft changed more than the mission of the book. He opened my mind and pushed me into a larger and more consequential arena. Also, he doesn't play fair. When we disagreed about something, he would use my writing against me, quoting concepts in the book to demonstrate my own limited thinking.

A great developmental editor helps authors find their voice. A great copyeditor represents the voice of the reader. Leslie Tilley sharpened my writing and always kept the experience of the reader front and center. I am struck by the range of Leslie's abilities. Her discerning eye took in everything from the coherence of my arguments to the accuracy of my references.

I'm grateful to Laura Duffy and Elina Cohen, who gave a work by an independent author the look and feel of a traditionally published book. My thanks to Susan Moxley and Mike Oppenheim for putting the finishing touches on the book with great care and efficiency.

I am indebted to Interaction Associates for the tools of my trade. The Interaction Method has equipped me to reach for my most noble aspirations. I have learned the art and science of facilitation from working alongside pioneers and world-class practitioners: Nancy Brodsky, Linda Dunkel, Peter Gibb, Kathi Joy, Thomas Rice, Barry Rosen, David Straus, and Marybeth Tahar. A few of my colleagues dared to bring the four disciplines to their clients even before we settled on how to turn the concept into a teachable, practical methodology. I'm very grateful to Beth O'Neill, Michael Reidy, and Beth Yates for experimenting with the disciplines and helping me understand how to spread the word.

I imposed early thoughts about this work on generous people. We met in airports, hotels, restaurants, coffee shops, corporate offices. More recently we connected by phone and by Zoom. Conversations with my creative, insightful, super-smart colleagues honed and polished the ideas described in this book. I am lucky and thankful to have people in my life with a passion for exploring ideas and a way of listening that brings out the best thinking in others. I hope that the following people recognize the impact of their thinking in how I have expressed the ideas in this book: Andy Atkins, Louise DeIasi, Marilyn Deming, Carolyn Fischer, Debra France, Meg Graham, Michele Gravelle, Chris Holliday, Kristin Leydig Bryant, Ursula Liff, Allison Manswell, Mia Mbroh, Neil Meyrick, Nick Noyes, Michael Reidy, Tracy Rickard, Lacy Roberson, Barry Rosen, Sara Shinneman, Angie Sifferman, and Jean Williams.

I want to single out a few close friends who continue to be reliable and enthusiastic thought partners: Joseph Alonzo, Nancy Brodsky, Kevin Cuthbert, Tim Goodman, Ford Hatamiya, and Lacy Roberson. They have witnessed my course reversals and listened patiently as I talked myself into a corner or thought in circles. They each share a stake in the ongoing mission to create openings for creativity and compassion when people feel stuck.

It's hard to sum up the value I've derived from people who took the time to read and comment on an advanced draft of the preface and the manuscript. I have learned important lessons about how to share my thinking. Readers have ended up with a clearer, more focused book. I'm grateful for the stunning generosity of Lisa Baird, Dave Brazel, Nancy Brodsky, Kevin Cuthbert, Kristi Erickson, Debra France, Samantha Goldstein, LeeAnn Mallory, Anne Mounts, Nancy Southern, and Lisa Stornaielo.

I want to acknowledge the clients who provided early opportunities to share the ideas in this book with leaders in their organizations: Leiza Brock, Mary Jo Coronado, Laura Eigel, Ed Garrison, Susan Hamilton, Sharon Hazard, Jen Hutcheson, Jennifer Large, Parinaz Sekechi, Jill Smith Tuttle, and Lori Whinery.

I feel the ever-present support of some very important women in my life. My mother Rosalie set me striving from an early age. Three older sisters—Judi Schindler, Carole Bonnet, and Ann Cone-Sevi—taught me how to pay attention and how to prevail at dinner-table storytelling. Katherine, my loving and caring partner in life, has kept me grounded for over 30 years. Nothing I accomplish gets done without her support, empathy, and generosity. Katherine wakes up every day thinking about the needs of others and how she can best be of service. Our daughters, Abby, Hannah, and Bekah, inspire and educate me. I'm most grateful to them for not letting me take myself too seriously.

Finally, Lisa Weaver, my business partner and life coach, has been a reliable safeguard against my unproductive perfectionism and pointless philosophizing. She compensates for my melancholy with an audacious confidence in the power of our work.

Your Unstuck Minds Profile

For the last few years, people learning about the four disciplines of an unstuck mind have started by taking an assessment called the Unstuck Minds Profile (UMP).

The UMP identifies what I refer to as your thinking-to-action preference. You can take the free assessment by visiting www.unstuckminds.com. If you have taken personality profiles or style assessments like the Big Five, or MBTI, or DiSC in the past, it's important to clarify what the UMP does and does not assess. Your thinking-to-action preference is not a description of your personality. Your UMP won't help you understand what energizes you or how you like to communicate or make decisions. Your UMP scores won't describe your general problem-solving style, but it will help you identify the type of information you're attracted to when trying to get oriented to a complex or uncertain challenge.

In addition to classifying your thinking-to-action preference, the UMP will help you understand the strength of your preference. Some people have strong preferences for certain types of information regardless of the situation that has them stuck. For others, the nature of the situation dictates the type of information they want. The UMP will indicate whether your style is more rigid, indicating a strong preference for certain information to the exclusion of seeking other information, or more agile, indicating a preference for varying the thought process based on the nature of the situation.

Whether you take the online assessment to learn about your thinking-to-action tendencies or simply reflect on how you get started when faced with a challenging situation, you will benefit from developing an awareness of your thinking habits. When you read the overviews of each style in the four sections that follow, consider which of them describes the information-gathering strategy that feels the most familiar and comfortable. Remember, you'll know that you have approached a challenge from all angles if you have reduced the risk of missing something important, avoided solving the wrong problem, discovered previously excluded perspectives, and generated new options.

INTERPRETING YOUR FOUR-DISCIPLINES SCORES: HOW YOU LIKE TO GET UNSTUCK

1. Explore the context

To get unstuck, people who start by exploring the context are drawn to changes in the external environment and emerging trends. An inclination to explore the context implies a preference for understanding what surrounds a situation. Exploring context is about noticing factors that we don't control but that nevertheless influence what has created our situations, what is changing about our situations, and what might be emerging as an opportunity worth our consideration.

When faced with a dissatisfying situation or when pursuing an opportunity in uncharted territory, people with an inclination to explore the context want to know what is changing. They pay attention to social and technological trends. They detect patterns that lead them to make predictions about the future. They build theories to explain the emergence of trends.

People inclined to explore context often work back from the preferred end state in order to set direction or prioritize next steps. They find it difficult to hear an analysis of recommendations about changing the current situation without first hearing about the big picture. They want to know why a topic became a priority and how solving it contributes to larger goals. They are attracted to questions concerning goals and strategy.

People with lower scores on the Explore dimension are distracted by a focus on context. When they feel stuck, they are not likely to look for answers outside of the team, function, or organization. They may feel impatient with conversations that seem overly theoretical or conceptual. They prefer to get unstuck by talking through relevant examples or concrete next steps.

People distracted by context are not helped by presentations that lay out the pros and cons of multiple options. When asking for criteria or success metrics, they don't want to hear *it depends*. They prefer to work within the constraints. They want to know what is in scope and what is out of scope. They may even feel that in some circumstances, it's best to just try something and learn from what happens.

2. Analyze structures

To get unstuck, people who start by analyzing structures are drawn to facts, data, and cause-and-effect relationships. An inclination to analyze structures implies a preference for understanding the systems and mindsets responsible for a situation. Analyzing structures is about noticing relationships among the elements of a system and the influences of habits, operating norms, and culture.

When faced with a dissatisfying situation or when pursuing an opportunity in uncharted territory, people with an inclination to analyze structures start by gathering facts. They want to understand the nature of the situation and may attempt to grasp what is happening by comparing the current state to what they have experienced in the past. Early in the process of getting unstuck, they will want to know what has happened that has led to the current situation.

People attracted to structures are interested in explanations that connect causes to effects. If data is available about the current situation, they will be eager to learn about trends, patterns, correlations, and aberrations. They may feel uncomfortable being asked to pursue a vague opportunity without boundary conditions or criteria for success. They are attracted to questions that establish clarity and constraints.

People with lower scores on the Analyze dimension are distracted by a focus on detail. When they feel stuck, they are not likely to seek out data and facts to help them get oriented. In fact, they may believe that facts and data could be misleading because they are rooted in what has already happened. They may also believe that adherence to the status quo may be part of the problem.

People distracted by detailed analysis may lose patience with presentations that quantify everything while offering no real insights into the nature of the situation. They suspect that something has changed, which renders traditional analysis and methods ineffectual. They would prefer to hear people's opinions and learn about emerging trends that could impact the organization's strategy and priorities.

3. Empathize with needs

To get unstuck, those who start by empathizing with needs are drawn to people, their perspectives, and their motivations. An inclination to empathize with needs implies a preference for understanding the nature of people's involvement in a situation. Empathizing with needs is about noticing the relationship between people's behaviors and their motivations. Empathizing with needs is also about noticing perspectives that are missing or underrepresented.

When faced with a dissatisfying situation or when pursuing an opportunity in uncharted territory, those with an inclination to empathize with needs want input from a variety of people. They want to understand the dynamics created by organizational politics. They recognize that nothing changes if people are unwilling or unprepared to adopt new behaviors.

They often ask presenters about who was involved in providing input to an analysis. When hearing about an implementation plan, they are likely to recommend a more robust communication and change-management strategy than the one being described. They are attracted to questions about people's inner lives.

People with lower scores on the Empathize dimension are distracted by a focus on the inner lives of stakeholders. When they feel stuck, they don't seek out a variety of opinions. They believe that a high-quality or highly creative option should take priority over a popular option. They can be suspicious of giving too much weight to the perspectives of stakeholders, reasoning that most people are focused on their own needs or agenda. If they are going to be swayed by an opinion, they prefer to hear from a recognized external expert.

People distracted by a focus on needs often think that employee engagement and employee satisfaction surveys are given too much emphasis when making strategic decisions. If the organization needs the cooperation of people to get unstuck, they would rather talk about incentives and performance metrics than about how people may be thinking and feeling when they hear about an upcoming change. They may even feel that in some circumstances it's in everyone's best interest to disrupt the status quo with a quick implementation of a big change.

4. Challenge assumptions

To get unstuck, people who start by challenging assumptions get curious about the way people are thinking about the situation. An inclination to challenge assumptions implies a preference for surfacing and questioning worldviews. People who challenge assumptions often approach problem-solving with an inherent skepticism about how a situation has been framed and the methodologies being employed to respond to the situation.

When faced with a dissatisfying situation or when pursuing an opportunity in uncharted territory, people with an inclination to challenge assumptions want to know why it's important to make a change. They pay attention to which thinking skills have been employed in getting oriented to the situation and which thinking skills may be underutilized. They might offer a disruptive suggestion or a seemingly impractical idea at the onset of a discussion just to gauge reactions. They are attracted to questions no one else is asking.

People with lower scores on the Challenge Assumptions dimension are distracted by theoretical or conceptual analysis of a situation. When they feel stuck, they get frustrated by hearing a variety of hypotheses about what is "really going on." They would prefer to take direction from an authority figure or use an established methodology as a way to make progress. Giving consideration to wild, impractical ideas feels to them like a waste of time.

People distracted by theory feel impatient during discussions of psychology or philosophy; they equate progress with action. They feel comfortable with the status quo and generally agree with the saying "If it ain't broke, don't fix it." They think that teams and organizations get stuck when they get distracted by "shiny new objects" and lose focus.

NOTES

Preface

1. While the original bystander recording showed Chauvin kneeling on Floyd's neck for 8 minutes and 46 seconds, footage from the other officers' body cameras that was released later revealed that the actual duration was 9 minutes, 30 seconds. Haley Willis, Evan Hill, Robin Stein, Christiaan Triebert, Ben Laffin, and Drew Jordan, "New Footage Shows Delayed Medical Response to George Floyd," *New York Times* (August 11, 2020; updated September 14, 2020), https://www.nytimes.com/2020/08/11/us/george-floyd-body-cam-full-video.html.

PART ONE: THE NATURE OF OUR INABILITY TO DEAL WITH CHAOS

Peter Drucker, *Managing in Turbulent Times* (New York: Routledge, 2011), x.

Chapter 1 / Redefining Problems

1. David Straus, *How to Make Collaboration Work: Powerful Ways to Build Consensus, Solve Problems, and Make Decisions* (San Francisco: Berrett-Koehler, 2002), 19.

2. Daniel Kahneman and Amos Tverksy, "Subjective Probability: A Judgment of Representativeness," *Cognitive Psychology* 3, no. 3 (July 1972), 430–454, https://doi.org/10.1016/0010-0285(72)90016-3.

3. Arie W. Kruglanski, *The Psychology of Closed-Mindedness: Essays in Social Psychology* (New York: Psychology Press, 2004).

4. Sander Koole and Klaus Rothermund, eds., *The Psychology of Implicit Emotion Regulation: A Special Issue of Cognition and Emotion* 25, no. 3 (New York: Psychology Press, 2011).

Chapter 2 / Are You Ever Surprised by How Often You're Right?

1. Scott Plous, *The Psychology of Judgment and Decision Making* (New York: McGraw Hill, 1993), 233.

2. Chris Argyris, *Overcoming Organizational Defenses: Facilitating Organizational Learning* (London: Pearson, 1990), 88–89.

Chapter 3 / Our Need for Closure

1. Else Frenkel-Brunswik, "Intolerance of Ambiguity as an Emotional and Perceptual Personality Variable," *Journal of Personality* 18 (September 1949), 108–143.

2. Four studies of ambiguity tolerance and its impacts:
Stanley Budner, "Intolerance of Ambiguity as a Personality Variable," *Journal of Personality* 30, no. 29 (March 1962), 29–50, https://doi.org/10.1111/j.1467-6494.1962.tb02303.x.
Adrian Furnham and Joseph Marks, "Tolerance of Ambiguity: A Review of the Recent Literature," *Psychology* 4, no. 9 (September 2013), 717–728.
Adrian Furnham and Tracy Ribchester, "Tolerance of Ambiguity: A Review of the Concept, Its Measurement and Applications," *Current Psychology* 14, no. 3 (September 1995), 179–199, https://doi.org/10.1007/BF02686907.
A. Keenan and G. D. M. McBain, "Effects of Type A Behaviour, Intolerance of Ambiguity, and Locus of Control on the Relationship between Role Stress and Work-Related Outcomes," *Journal of Occupational Psychology* 52, no. 4 (December 1979), 277–285, https://doi.org/10.1111/j.2044-8325.1979.tb00462.

3. Kruglanski, *The Psychology of Closed-Mindedness*, 6.

4. Antonia Chirumbolo, et al., "Motivated Closed-Mindedness and Creativity in Small Groups," *Small Group Research* 36, no. 1 (February 2005), 59–82, https://doi.org/10.1177/1046496404268535.

5. Alain Van Hiel and Ivan Mervielde, "Effects of Ambiguity and Need for Closure on the Acquisition of Information," *Social Cognition* 20, no. 5 (October 2002), 380–408, https://doi.org/10.1521/soco.20.5.380.21126.

6. Arie W. Kruglanski and Donna M. Webster, "Motivated Closing of the Mind: 'Seizing' and 'Freezing'," *Psychological Review* 103, No. 2 (March 1996), 263–283, https://doi.org/10.1037/0033-295X.103.2.263.

Chapter 4 / Immunity to Change

1. William Bridges, *Managing Transitions: Making the Most of Change* (Reading, MA: Perseus Books, 1991).

2. Daniel Kahneman, *Thinking, Fast and Slow* (New York: Farrar, Straus, and Giroux, 2011), 283.

3. Kahneman, 284.

4. Kahneman, 305.

5. Jonas T. Kaplan, Sarah I. Gimbel, and Sam Harris, "Neural Correlates of Maintaining One's Political Beliefs in the Face of Counterevidence," *Scientific Reports* 6, no. 39589 (December 2016), 8, https://doi.org/10.1038/srep39589.

6. David Bauder, "Fox News Channel Viewers Tune Out for John Lewis' Funeral," *AP NEWS* (August 4, 2020), https://apnews.com/a7f2d9f88e22f35dbc85fcfd2f54f386.

7. "Largest Federal Workers Union Decries Administration Efforts to Undermine Diversity and Inclusion Training in Federal Government" (AFGE press release, September 5, 2020), https://www.afge.org/publication/largest-federal-workers-union-decries-administration-efforts-to-undermine-diversity-and-inclusion-training-in-federal-government.

8. Jack Mezirow, ed., *Learning as Transformation: Critical Perspectives on a Theory in Progress* (San Francisco: Jossey-Bass, 2009).

9. Robert Kegan and Lisa Laskow Lahey, *Immunity to Change: How to Overcome It and Unlock the Potential in Yourself and Your Organization* (Boston: Harvard University Press, 2009).

Chapter 5 / Organizations Can Also Become Immune to Change

1. Sam Levin, "Netflix co-founder: 'Blockbuster Laughed at Us … Now There's One Left'," *The Guardian* (September 14, 2019), https://www.theguardian.com/media/2019/sep/14/netflix-marc-randolph-founder-blockbuster.

2. Scott D. Anthony, "Kodak's Downfall Wasn't About Technology," *Harvard Business Review* (July 15, 2016), https://hbr.org/2016/07/kodaks-downfall-wasnt-about-technology.

Chapter 6 / When Blind Spots and Threats Join Forces

1. Keith Johnstone, *Impro for Storytellers* (New York: Routledge, 1999), 59.

2. Kerwin Swint, "Adams vs. Jefferson: The Birth of Negative Campaigning in the U.S.," Mental Floss (September 9, 2012), https://www.mentalfloss.com/article/12487/adams-vs-jefferson-birth-negative-campaigning-us.

PART TWO: THE BEGINNER'S MIND

Shunryu Suzuki, *Zen Mind, Beginner's Mind: Informal Talks on Zen Meditation and Practice, 50th Anniversary Edition* (Boulder, CO: Shambhala, 2020), 2.

Chapter 7 / Using My Useless Degree

1. Robert Johnson and Adam Cureton, "Kant's Moral Philosophy," Stanford Encyclopedia of Philosophy Archive, ed. Edward N. Zalta, (Spring 2019 edition), https://plato.stanford.edu/archives/spr2019/entries/kant-moral/.

2. Joan P. Kerr, "What Good Is a New-born Baby?" *American Heritage* 25, no. 1 (December 1973), https://www.americanheritage.com/what-good-new-born-baby.

3. "quodlibetic," *Merriam-Webster* https://www.merriam-webster.com/dictionary/quodlibetic.

Chapter 8 / Cultivating a Beginner's Mind

1. Carol S. Dweck, *Mindset: The New Psychology of* Success (New York: Ballantine, 2006).

2. Keith L. Lindblom, *Edwin Land and Instant Photography* (Washington, D.C.: American Chemical Society, 2015), https://www.acs.org/content/dam/acsorg/education/whatischemistry/landmarks/landinstantphotography/edwin-land-polaroid-booklet.pdf.

3. Roger L. Martin, "How Successful Leaders Think," *Harvard Business Review* 85, no. 6 (June 2007), 60–67.

4. Martin, 62.

5. F. Scott Fitzgerald, "The Crack-Up," in *The Crack-Up: With Other Uncollected Pieces, Note-Books and Unpublished Letters*, ed. Edmund Wilson (New York: New Directions, 1956), 69.

6. "About Us," Lego Group, https://www.lego.com/en-us/aboutus/lego-group/the-lego-brand/.

7. Nicole Branan, "Are Our Brains Wired for Categorization?" *Scientific American Mind,* (January 1, 2010), https://www.scientificamerican.com/article/wired-for-categorization/.

8. Christie Wilcox, "What's in a Name? Taxonomy Problems Vex Biologists," *Quanta Magazine* (June 24, 2019), https://www.quantamagazine.org/phyla-and-other-flawed-taxonomic-categories-vex-biologists-20190624/.

9. Ryan Lizza and Daniel Lippman, "Wearing a Mask Is for Smug Liberals. Refusing to Is for Reckless Republicans," *Politico* (May 1, 2020), https://www.politico.com/news/2020/05/01/masks-politics-coronavirus-227765.

10. Lina Zeldovich, "The Evolution of 'Autism' as a Diagnosis, Explained," Spectrum (May 9, 2018), https://www.spectrumnews.org/news/evolution-autism-diagnosis-explained/.

11. Lou Stoppard, "Will Mandatory Face Masks End the Burqa Bans?" *New York Times* (May 19, 2020), https://www.nytimes.com/2020/05/19/style/face-mask-burqa-ban.html.

Chapter 9 / Question-ability

1. Albert Einstein, statement to William Miller, "Old Man's Advice to Youth: 'Never Lose a Holy Curiosity.'" *Life* (May 2, 1955), 64.

2. Thomas Wedell-Wedellsborg, *What's Your Problem? To Solve Your Toughest Problems, Change the Problems You Solve* (Boston: Harvard Business Review Press, 2020), 5–6.

3. Hal Gregersen, *Questions Are the Answer: A Breakthrough Approach to Your Most Vexing Problems at Work and in Life* (New York: HarperCollins, 2018), 12.

4. Ronald A. Heifetz and Marty Linsky*, Leadership on the Line: Staying Alive Through the Dangers of Leading* (Boston: Harvard Business Review Press, 2002), 53.

5. IBM Annual Report: 1994, 2, https://www.ibm.com/investor/att/pdf/IBM_Annual_Report_1994.pdf.

6. Louis V. Gerstner, Jr., *Who Says Elephants Can't Dance: Leading a Great Enterprise Through Dramatic Change* (New York: HarperCollins, 2002), 44.

7. Carroll Doherty, "Key Takeaways on Americans' Growing Partisan Divide Over Political Values," Pew Research Center (October 5, 2017), https://www.pewresearch.org/fact-tank/2017/10/05/takeaways-on-americans-growing-partisan-divide-over-political-values/.

8. Ezra Klein, *Why We're Polarized* (New York: Simon & Schuster, 2020), 13.

Chapter 10 / The Downside of Expertise

1. Lewis Carroll, *Alice's Adventures in Wonderland* (New York: Maynard, Merrill, 1895), 50–51.

2. Holly Yan, "Top Health Officials Have Changed Their Minds About Face Mask Guidance—But for Good Reason," CNN Health (July 20, 2020), https://www.cnn.com/2020/07/19/health/face-masks-us-guidance/index.html

3. Eric Hoffer, *Reflections on the Human Condition* (New York: Harper & Row, 1973), 22.

PART THREE: FOUR DISCIPLINES FOR NAVIGATING CHAOS

David Mitchell, *Utopia Avenue* (New York: Random House, 2020), 454.

Chapter 12 / Introduction to the Four Disciplines

1. The "sell more pens" exercise is based on a similar exercise developed by Edwin C. Selby, Donald J. Treffinger, and Scott G. Isaksen, authors of VIEW: An Assessment of Problem-Solving Style, https://www.viewassessment.com/.

Chapter 13 / Discipline 1: Explore the Context

1. Matt Mullenweg, "Automattic, Forbes, and the Future of Work," ma.tt (September 5, 2020), https://ma.tt/2012/09/future-of-work/.

2. Philip Roth, *The Plot Against America* (New York: Houghton Mifflin Harcourt, 2004).

Chapter 14 / Discipline 2: Analyze Structures

1. W.E.B. Du Bois, *The World and Africa* (New York: Oxford University Press, 2007), 212.

2. Geert Hofstede, Gert Jan Hofstede, and Michael Minkov, *Cultures and Organizations: Software of the Mind,* 3rd ed. (New York: McGraw-Hill, 2013.

3. Robert Dallek, "JFK vs. the Military," *The Atlantic* (Fall 2013), https://www.theatlantic.com/magazine/archive/2013/08/jfk-vs-the-military/309496/.

Chapter 15 / Discipline 3: Empathize with Needs

1. Theodore Levitt, *The Marketing Mode: Pathways to Corporate Growth* (New York: McGraw-Hill, 1969), 1.

2. Richard Fisher, William Ury, and Bruce Patton (ed.), *Getting to Yes: Negotiating Agreement Without Giving In* (Boston: Houghton Mifflin, 1981), 40–55.

3. Tim Brown, *Change by Design: How Design Thinking Transforms Organizations and Inspires Innovation* (New York: HarperCollins, 2009), 44.

4. Tara Westover, *Educated: A Memoir* (New York: Random House, 2018).

5. Chimamanda Ngozi Adichie, "The Danger of a Single Story," TED (2009), https://www.ted.com/talks/chimamanda_ngozi_adichie_the_danger_of_a_single_story?language=en

6. Will Schutz, *The Human Element: Productivity, Self-Esteem, and the Bottom Line* (San Francisco: Jossey-Bass, 1994), 31.

7. Charles Duhigg, "What Google Learned From Its Quest to Build the Perfect Team," *New York Times Magazine* (February 25, 2016), https://www.nytimes.com/2016/02/28/magazine/what-google-learned-from-its-quest-to-build-the-perfect-team.html.

8. Amy Edmondson, "Psychological Safety and Learning Behavior in Work Teams," *Administrative Science Quarterly* 44, no. 2 (June 1999), 350–83, https://doi.org/10.2307/2666999.

9. Brené Brown, "The Power of Vulnerability," TED (June 2010), https://www.ted.com/talks/brene_brown_the_power_of_vulnerability?language=en.

Chapter 16 / Discipline 4: Challenge Assumptions

1. For a description of a successful reverse mentorship program at Estee Lauder, see Emma Sandler, "How The Estee Lauder Companies Is Tapping Its Millennial and Gen-Z Employees to Modernize," Glossy (February 13, 2019), https://www.glossy.co/beauty/how-the-estee-lauder-companies-is-using-millennials-and-gen-z-to-modernize-its-corporate-structure.

2. Charles Albert Eric Goodhart, *Monetary Theory and Practice: The UK Experience* (New York: Macmillan, 1984).

3. Tony Greenwald, Mahzarin Banaji, and Brian Nosek, Project Implicit, https://www.projectimplicit.net/.

4. Jeffery DelViscio, "A Nixon Deepfake, a 'Moon Disaster' Speech and an Information Ecosystem at Risk," *Scientific American* (July 20, 2020), https://www.scientificamerican.com/article/a-nixon-deepfake-a-moon-disaster-speech-and-an-information-ecosystem-at-risk1/.

Chapter 17 / Restoring Creativity and Compassion

1. Victor Frankl, *Man's Search for Meaning* (New York: Simon & Schuster, 1959), 86.

INDEX

INDEX

Mattel, 64
McGivena, Leo, 126
meetings, 114
Mendela, Nelson, 60
Mervielde, Ivan, 27
metrics, 140–141
Mezirow, Jack, 36
Mindset (Dweck), 60–61
MIT Leadership Center, 70
Mitchell, David, 97
Mullenweg, Matt, 106
multitasking, 118–119
Muslims, 49, 66–67

national cultures, 116–117
National Institute of Allergy
    and Infectious Diseases,
    81
needs, 124–126
negative campaigns, 49
Netflix, 40–41
neuroscience, 34, 39
Nixon, Richard, 146–147
Nosek, Brian, 144–145

Oakland Raiders, 122
Obama, Barack, 35
opinion leaders, 108
organizational leaders
    behavior of, 85–86
    Cambridge Leadership Associates
        for, 71
    collaboration with, 42–43
    customer needs for, 123
    decision-making for, 30
    getting unstuck for, 7
    knowledge for, 75
    learning for, 63–64
    promotions and, 56
    psychology of, 18–19
    uncertainty for, 1, 75–76
    Unstuck Minds for, 5
organizations
    arguments in, 124–125
    change for, 40–43
    decision-making by, 100–101

getting stuck for, 133
goals for, 103–104
promotions in, 73–74
question-ability for, 68–77
shareholders of, 109
outliers, 128–129

paralysis, 14, 29–30, 67
partisanship, 76–77
patterns, 112, 114, 118
perception, 84–85
performance appraisals, 56
peripheries, 133
permanence tendency, 29–30
personification, of systems,
    122–123
perspectives, 94, 107, 133–134
pessimism, 6
Pew Research Center, 76
philosophy, 54–55, 57–58, 70,
    80–81, 91–92, 113
The Plot Against America (Roth),
    110
Plous, Scott, 19
Polaroid Corporation, 61–62
politics, 1–3, 7
    categorization in, 65
    Covid-19 and, 150
    Inquiry Loop model for,
        49–50
    partisanship in, 76–77
    political beliefs, 34
    political identity, 16–17
    in United States, 48–49
potential consequences, 121–122
"The Power of Vulnerability"
    (Brown, B.), 135
problems
    analysis of, 112–114
    arguments and, 93–94
    with expertise, 78–83
    from feeling stuck, 23–24
    framing of, 86
    identification of, 114
    redefining, 11–17
    with scholarship, 99–100

ABOUT UNSTUCK MINDS

Unstuck Minds helps people access creativity and compassion when they feel stuck. We operate as a network of practitioners who believe that organizations and communities thrive when they learn to unlock the potential of people. Unstuck Minds offers workshops, consulting services, and executive coaching.

Our work focuses on recognizing and avoiding the thinking traps that obscure insights and limit options. When people feel stuck, they grow more isolated and divided. When people get unstuck, their breakthroughs restore the confidence and momentum that allow them to take concerted action. Unstuck Minds has used the four disciplines described in this book to help organizations around the world form strategies, design more inclusive cultures, and teach their leaders to be more agile and adaptable.

Learn more by visiting www.unstuckminds.com.

ABOUT THE AUTHOR

JAY GORDON CONE teaches people how to think together and solve problems together. Jay has spent the past 35 years supporting leadership development and organizational change. He has worked with leaders and organizations around the world.

Jay is a founding partner of Unstuck Minds, a firm focused on helping people access creativity and compassion when they feel stuck. Before starting Unstuck Minds with his business partner, Lisa Weaver, Jay spent 20 years as a senior consultant for Interaction Associates. Prior to that, Jay held a number of talent development, human resources, and organizational development roles in the food service industry.

Jay served for five years as adjunct faculty for the Executive MBA program at The University of Texas at Dallas. He has written extensively about organizational leadership and strategy. His articles have appeared in *Training Magazine, Training & Development Journal,* and *Global Business and Organizational Excellence.* Jay authored the chapter "Authentic Accountability" in the International Leadership Association's 2011 collection, *Leadership for Transformation.* His article "How to Cultivate an Unstuck Mind" was featured in the Fall 2019 issue of *Rotman Management Magazine.*

His current and past clients include The Bill and Melinda Gates Foundation, Dell Technologies, Exelon, GE, Nokia, Fluor Corporation, The TJX Companies, and W.L. Gore and Associates.

Jay and his wife, Katherine, live in Dallas, Texas. They have three adult daughters: Abby, Hannah, and Bekah.